Fourth edition

Project

Student's Book

1

OXFORD

Tom Hutchinson

Contents

1 Introduction

1A Hello

Hi! My name's Ravi Gupta.

Hello. My name's Carla Fletcher.

Hello. I'm Molly Dawson.

Hello. I'm Joe Bradley.

Hi! I'm Mel Bradley.

And I'm Andy Fletcher.

Hi! I'm Mickey.

I'm Millie.

And I'm Mut. What's your name?

1 a 🎧 1.2 **Read and listen.**

b 🎧 1.2 **Listen again and repeat.**

2 Ask and answer.

Who's this?

It's Ravi Gupta.

3 🎧 1.3 **Listen. Who do you hear? Write the names.**

1 *Carla* and *Joe*.
2 Andy Fletcher, Mrs Williams and _____.
3 Carla, _____ and _____.
4 Molly and _____.
5 _____, _____ and _____.

4 Work in a group. Introduce yourself.

- *Hello. I'm _____. What's your name?*
- *My name's _____.*

5 a 🎧 1.4 **Listen and repeat.**

Hello.
Hi!
Good morning.
Good afternoon.
Good evening.

Goodbye.
Bye.
See you later.
See you.

Good night.

b 🎧 1.5 **Listen and answer.**

● *Good morning.*
○ *Good morning.*

c Work with a partner. Make dialogues. Use different expressions.

● *Good morning.*
○ *Hello.*

6 a 🎧 1.6 **Read and listen. Complete the dialogues.**

Molly	¹_____, Andy.
Andy	Oh, ²_____, Molly. How are you?
Molly	I'm fine, thanks. And you?
Andy	Fine.
Molly	OK. ³_____.
Andy	Yes. ⁴_____.

Carla	Good ⁵_____, Mr Walker. How are you?
Mr Walker	⁶_____, Carla. I'm fine, thanks. And ⁷_____?
Carla	I'm ⁸_____, thank you, sir.
Mr Walker	That's ⁹_____.
Carla	¹⁰_____ you later, sir.
Mr Walker	Yes. ¹¹_____, Carla.

b Work with a partner. Read the dialogue.

c Go round the class. Make new dialogues. Use different expressions.

1B In the classroom

1 🎧 1.7 **Read and listen.**

a book **an** apple

Why is it a book, but an apple?

Vocabulary

2 a Complete the labels with *a* or *an*.

3 🎧 1.9 **Listen. Draw the thing that you hear.**

- *What's this?*
- *It's an umbrella.*

Speaking

4 Work with a partner. Ask and answer about things in your classroom.

What's this?

It's an apple.

1 *a* board
2 _____ picture
3 _____ house
4 _____ man
5 _____ woman
6 _____ cat
7 _____ dog
8 _____ window
9 _____ orange
10 _____ door
11 _____ chair
12 _____ pen
13 _____ pencil
14 _____ desk
15 _____ bag
16 _____ watch
17 _____ umbrella
18 _____ exercise book
19 _____ boy
20 _____ girl

b 🎧 1.8 **Listen and repeat.**

Vocabulary

5 a 🎧 1.10 **Read the instructions. Listen and repeat.**

1 Read.

2 Say 'Good morning'.

3 Open your exercise book.

4 Listen.

5 Draw.

6 Put down your pencil.

7 Close your exercise book.

8 Pick up your pencil.

9 Sit down.

10 Look at the picture.

11 Go to the board.

12 Stand up.

13 Write on the board.

14 Come here.

15 Give me your book, please.

b 🎧 1.10 **Listen again and do the actions.**

Grammar

6 🎧 1.11 **Look at Millie and Mut. Then listen and say the negative.**

Listening and speaking

7 🎧 1.12 **Listen and follow the new instructions.**

8 Give a partner some instructions.

Listen.

Don't listen.

1C Numbers

Vocabulary

1 a Write the words in the correct order.

| two seven oh (zero) nine one |
| six ten three five four eight |

Numbers 0–10

0 oh (zero)   **6** ____

1 one   **7** ____

2 ____   **8** ____

3 ____   **9** ____

4 ____   **10** ____

5 ____

b **1.13** **Listen, check and repeat.**

Comprehension

2 a **1.14** **Read and listen. Complete the phone numbers.**

Andy   _ 4 _ _ 0 _
Mel   0 _ _ 0 0 9 _ 1 _ 7 _

What's your phone number, Andy?

It's six four double eight oh two.

What's your mobile number, Mel?

It's oh double seven double oh, nine three one, four seven five.

b Work with a partner. Read the dialogues.

3 a **1.15** **Listen. Write the phone numbers.**

Name	phone number
John	511698
Katie	
Sanjit	
Laura	

b Ask and answer with a partner. Use the phone numbers. Ask and answer.

- *What's your telephone number, John?*
- *It's five double one six nine eight.*

4 Collect five phone numbers from people in your class.

Vocabulary

5 **1.16** **Listen and repeat.**

11 eleven	**30** thirty
12 twelve	**40** forty
13 thirteen	**50** fifty
14 fourteen	**60** sixty
15 fifteen	**70** seventy
16 sixteen	**80** eighty
17 seventeen	**90** ninety
18 eighteen	**100** a hundred
19 nineteen	
20 twenty	

Look. Be careful! fourteen forty

6 a Read the numbers.

b 🎧 1.17 Listen. Which number do you hear?

7 Continue the numbers. Count round the class.

20 *twenty*

   21 *twenty-one*

      22 *twenty-two*

         23 *twenty-three*

            24 .....

8 Say the numbers.

22 39 41 53 67 76 85 94

Listening and speaking

9 🎧 1.18 Listen. Write the numbers you hear.

71

10 Play Fizz Buzz. Work in a group and count. For all 'five' numbers (5, 10, 15, 20 …) say 'fizz'. For all 'seven' numbers (7, 14, 21, 28 …) say 'buzz'.

one, two, three, four, fizz, six, buzz, eight, nine, fizz, eleven, twelve, thirteen, buzz, fizz, sixteen …

11 a 🎧 1.19 Listen to the first part of the song.

> **This old man**
>
> *1* This old man he played *one*.
> He played knick knack *on my drum*.
> *Chorus*
> With a knick knack paddy whack,
> Give a dog a bone.
> This old man came rolling home.

b 🎧 1.20 Listen to the song. Put the pictures in the order you hear them.

> *2* This old man he played *two*.
> He played knick knack *on my shoe*.

☐ down a mine

☐ at my gate

☐ on my hive

☐ up a tree

☐ up in heaven

☐ with my pen

☐ on my shoe

☐ on my door

☐ with some sticks

c 🎧 1.21 Listen to the whole song and sing.

1D How do you spell that?

Vocabulary

1 🎧 1.22 Listen and repeat.

Aa Bb Cc Dd Ee Ff
Gg Hh Ii Jj Kk Ll Mm
Nn Oo Pp Qq Rr Ss Tt
Uu Vv Ww Xx Yy Zz

2 🎧 1.23 Listen and sing.

Let's sing the ABC.
Sing the letters, sing with me.
A B C D
E F G
H I J K
L M N O P
Q R S
T U V
W X Y and Z.
Let's sing the ABC.
Sing the letters, sing with me.

Let's sing the ABC.

3 🎧 1.24 Listen and write the words.

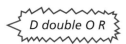

D double O R

1 door

4 a 🎧 1.22 Listen to the alphabet again. Put the letters in the column with the same sound.

/eɪ/	/ɪː/	/e/	/aɪ/	/əʊ/	/juː/	/ɑː/
A	B	F	I	O	Q	R
	C					

b 🎧 1.25 Listen and check.

c Say the letters in each column.

5 a Work with a partner. Spell some words.

b Work in a group. Spell your name.

Listening and speaking

6 a 🎧 1.26 Listen. Is the spelling correct? Correct the ones that are wrong.

1 ✓   5 _____
2 ✗ *window* 6 _____
3 _____   7 _____
4 _____   8 _____

b Test your partner with some words.

How do you spell …? *It's …*

Grammar

7 🎧 1.27 Look at the table. Listen and repeat.

How do we make plurals?

Singular	Plural
a dog	two dogs
a car	three cars
a book	four books

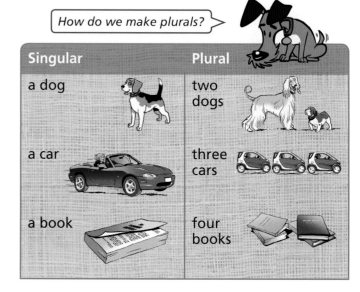

8 How many of these things are there in your classroom?

desks	windows	boys	girls
doors	pictures	chairs	bags

There are twenty desks.

9 🎧 1.28 **Listen and repeat.**

Be careful with these plurals.

Singular	Plural
an orange	two oranges
a watch	three watches
a glass	two glasses
a box	two boxes
a toothbrush	three toothbrushes
a man	two men
a woman	two women
a child	three children
a person	four people

Speaking and writing

10 a **What's in the picture?**

There's a cat.
There are four chairs.

b 🎧 1.29 **Close your book. Listen. Are the sentences true or false?**

There are two dogs in the picture.
False. There's only one dog.

c 🎧 1.29 **Open your book. Listen again and check your answers to exercise 10b.**

Names

1 a (1.30) **Read and listen.**

b Compare this to names in your country.

Hi. I'm Andy Fletcher. This is my full name.

Andrew Martin Fletcher

Andrew is my first name.

Martin is my middle name.

Fletcher is my surname.

My real name is Andrew, but people call me Andy. A lot of English names have short forms. Do you have short forms for names in your country?

My friends often call me 'Fletch'. It's a nickname. Do you have nicknames for your friends?

Hi, Fletch.

2 (1.31) **Read and listen. Write the short forms.**

Boys:		Girls:	
1 Christopher	> *Chris*	**1** Elizabeth	> _____
2 Michael	> _____	**2** Catherine	> _____
3 Thomas	> _____	**3** Megan	> _____

3 (1.32) **Read and listen to the people. Copy and complete the chart.**

	1	2
full name	Bradley Adam Grant	
short name	Brad	
nickname	Bags	

1

Hi. My full name is Bradley Adam Grant. Most people call me Brad. But my friends often call me Bags. It's a nickname from my initials: Bradley Adam Grant – B A G.

2

Hello. My name's Abigail Parker. Everyone calls me Abbie. That's short for Abigail. My middle name is Sophie. I haven't got a nickname.

3

Hello. I'm Tim Roberts. Actually my full name is Daniel Timothy Roberts. So Tim is short for my middle name, Timothy. (I use my middle name, because my dad's name is Daniel, too.) My nickname is Robbo – from my surname, Roberts.

4

Hi. My name's Jojo. It isn't my real name. It's a nickname. My full name is Joanna Megan Jones. So I'm Joanna Jones – Jojo. Only my friends call me Jojo. The teacher and my parents call me Joanna or Jo.

Maths: sums

1 🎧 1.33 **Look at the symbols. Listen and repeat.**

➕ plus

➖ minus

✖ times

➗ divided by

🟰 equals

2 a Write the missing symbols or numbers.

1	16	_+_	27	=	43
2	100	÷	4	=	___
3	87	-	___	=	74
4	12	x	8	=	___
5	68	___	17	=	4
6	34	___	29	=	63
7	23	___	4	=	92
8	99	-	66	=	___

b Say the sums aloud.

sixteen plus twenty-seven equals forty-three

3 Test a partner.

- *What's seven times five?*
- *Seven times five equals thirty-five.*

4 Look at the map and answer the questions.

1 Go from Birmingham to Derby and then to Nottingham. How far is it?

2 Go from Nottingham to Derby and back. How far is it?

3 Go from Coventry to Nottingham, and then to Birmingham. How far is it?

4 Go from Birmingham to Coventry and back three times. How far is it?

5 a Look at the picture. What are the scores for.

1 the yellow darts? 2 the green darts?
3 the blue darts?

b Which colour is the winner?

6 What is the answer?

| 1 | 6 | x5 | +2 | ÷4 | -7 | = | |
| 2 | 12 | +23 | +7 | -9 | x2 | = | 333 |

Conduct of Caron

Listening and speaking

1 🎧 (1.34) **Listen and correct the information about these two people.**

1
Name: _Kelly Harison_
Age: _12_
Telephone number:
_760442751_

2
Name: _Mark Foster_
Age: _12_
Telephone number:
_79460032_

2 a 🎧 (1.35) **What is the boy's name? What number is he in the competition?**

b 🎧 (1.35) **Listen again and complete the dialogue.**

A Good ¹_____. How are ²_____?
B I'm ³_____, thanks. And you?
A Fine. What's your ⁴_____?
B It's ⁵_____.
A How do you ⁶_____ that?
B It's ⁷__ __ __ __ __ __ __.
A Thank you. And what's your ⁸_____ name?
B ⁹_____
A Is that short for ¹⁰_____?
B ¹¹_____, it is.
A OK. You're number ¹²_____.
B ¹³_____ you.

In the classroom

3 **Copy the table. Put the words into the correct column.**

bag   pencil   door   window   cat   orange
boy   umbrella   girl   exercise book   picture
board   desk   apple

a	an

4 🎧 (1.36) **Listen and follow the instructions.**

Numbers

5 a **Say the numbers.**

27 32 13 51 80 18 39 15 40 4 100 6

b 🎧 (1.37) **Listen. Which numbers do you hear?**

Plurals

6 a **What's in the picture?**

There's a door.
There are two windows.

b **Look at the picture again. Write five sentences about it.**

There are four desks.

Your Project

Presenting your project

1 This is my project. It's on a poster.

My Life

This is my house. It's number 45.

This is my skateboard.

My favourite football team is Manchester United.

2 Ravi's project is on a computer.

My name's Ravi. My full name is Ravinder.

This is my bike.

My best friend is Andy Fletcher.

3 Make a project about your life.
1 Find pictures of people and things in your life.
2 Write speech bubbles and captions for your pictures
3 Put the things together to make a project.

Song

1 🎧 1.38 **Listen and sing.**

There were ten in the bed

There were ten in the bed
And the little one said,
Roll over, roll over.
So they all rolled over and
one fell out.

There were nine in the bed
And the little one said,
Roll over, roll over.
So they all rolled over and one fell out.
Repeat with 8, 7, 6, 5, 4, 3, 2

There was one in the bed
And the little one said,
Roll over, roll over.
So he rolled over and he fell out.
There were none in the bed
So no one said, Roll over, roll over.

ROLL OVER ROLL OVER

2 Friends and family

2A Where are you from?

Vocabulary

1 a 🎧 1.39 **Listen and repeat.**

 1 Britain
 7 Australia
 2 The USA
 8 Brazil
 3 France
 9 Italy
 4 China
 10 Russia
 5 Germany
 11 Greece
 6 Japan
 12 Spain

b **Find the countries on the map on pages 82 and 83. Find your country.**

2 a **Where are these cities? Reorder the words and complete the sentences.**

1 Tokyo is in *Japan. paanj*

2 Rio de Janeiro is in _____. *libzar*

3 Sydney is in _____. *aalsrutai*

4 Milan is in _____. *ilyat*

5 London is in _____. *natibir*

6 Paris is in _____. *racnef*

7 Moscow is in _____. *ssariu*

8 New York is in _____. *het sau*

9 Beijing is in _____. *nahci*

b 🎧 1.40 **Listen and check.**

Comprehension

3 Look at the pictures. Answer the questions.

1 Who are the boy and girl on the computer?

2 Where are they from?

Hi. I'm Mel Bradley. I'm from Britain. These are my Internet friends.

This is Max. He's thirteen. And this is Lauren. She's twelve. They're from the USA.

Hi. We're from New York.

4 🎧 1.41 **Here are some more of Mel's Internet friends. Listen. Which countries are the people from?**

1 Vera is from Rio de Janeiro.
She's from Brazil.

Grammar

5 a Look again at exercise 3. Copy and complete the table with **'s**, **'m**, or **'re**.

This is the verb be.

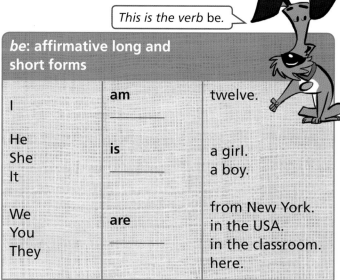

be: affirmative long and short forms

I	am	twelve.
	_____	
He		
She	is	a girl.
It	_____	a boy.
We		from New York.
You	are	in the USA.
They	_____	in the classroom.
		here.

b Make five sentences. Use the table.

6 a Complete the sentences with *am*, *is* or *are* and the name of the country.

1 This is Rosa. She _____ from
_____ ![flag]. She _____ eleven.

2 I _____ from _____ ![flag].
My name _____ Manuel and I _____
twelve.

3 We _____ from _____ ![flag].
We _____ from Sydney.

4 This is Hans. He _____ eleven and he
_____ from _____ ![flag].

5 They _____ from _____ ![flag].

b Change the sentences. Use the short forms.

7 a 🎧 1.42 Read and listen.

I'm not Mel. I'm Lauren.

*Lauren isn't twelve.
She's thirteen.
We aren't from Britain.
We're from the USA.*

b Copy and complete the table with the short forms.

be: negative long forms	short forms
I **am not** Mel.	I _____ Mel.
Max **is not** twelve.	Max _____ twelve.
We **are not** from Britain.	We _____ from Britain.

8 Make the sentences negative.

1 I'm from France.
I'm not from France.
2 She's twelve.
3 They're from London.
4 He's my friend.
5 We're from Greece.
6 I'm eleven.
7 My name's Joe.
8 Your friends are here.

Speaking and writing

9 Work in a group. Play a game.

A *I'm not from Australia.*
B *He isn't from Australia and I'm not from France.*

10 a Introduce yourself. Complete the sentences.

Hello. My name's [1]_____. I'm [2]_____ (age)
and I'm from [3]_____ (city) in [4]_____ (country).

b Introduce a famous person (a film star, a sportsperson, etc).

This is [5]_____. He's / She's [6]_____ (age)
and he's / she's from [7]_____ (city) in [8]_____
(country).

2B My family

Vocabulary

1 a 🎧 1.43 **Listen and repeat.**

b 🎧 1.44 **Listen. If the word you hear is male, stand up. If it's female, don't stand up.**

dad

Comprehension

2 🎧 1.45 **Read and listen. Answer the questions.**

1 Who are the people in the photo?
2 Where are they?

This is my family.

We're in our garden.

This is my mum. Her name's Mary.

This is my brother, Joe.

This is my dad. His name's Jack.

This is my grandma and my granddad.

And this is their dog. Its name's Buddy.

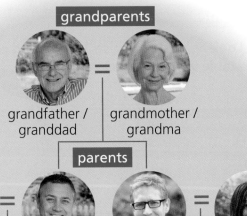

grandparents

grandfather / granddad   =   grandmother / grandma

parents

mother (mum)   =   father (dad)   uncle   =   aunt

children / grandchildren

daughter / sister   son / brother   cousin

These are possessive adjectives.

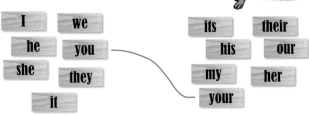

Grammar

3 Match the pronouns to the possessive adjectives.

I	we
he	you
she	they
it	

its	their
his	our
my	her
your	

4 Ask and answer about people in your class.

- *What's her name?*
- *Her name's Maria.*

- *What's his name?*
- *His name's Carl.*

5 Copy and complete the sentences with the possessive adjectives.

> **1** She's my mum. I'm _____ daughter.

> We're _____ children.

> They're _____ grandparents.

> He's _____ brother.

> I'm _____ son.

6 ⏺ 1.46 Read and listen.

This is Mel. This is her mobile.
This is Mel**'s** mobile.

> This is our house.

This is Joe and Mel**'s** house.

7 Whose is it? Write sentences.

This is Joe's toothbrush.

1 Joe
2 Mel
3 Jack
4 Mary
5 Grandma
6 Buddy
7 Uncle Tom
8 Auntie Julia

Listening and speaking

8 a ⏺ 1.47 Listen. Connect the things to the people.

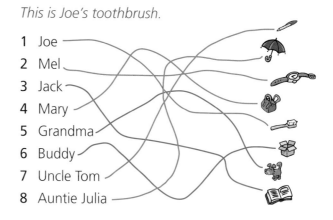

> Whose book is this?

b Work in a group. Each person puts three things on the table. In turns, pick up one thing and say whose it is.

This is Maria's watch.

Comprehension

1 a 🎧 1.48 **Read and listen. Choose the correct answers.**

1 Mickey and Millie's house is in:
  a London Road. b London Avenue.
2 The man is:
  a their neighbour. b a postman.

b Work in a group. Act the story.

Grammar

2 Copy and complete the table.

How do we make questions with be?

be: questions

This is London Road.

Is this London Road?

You are our new postman.

_____ you our new postman?

Your dog is friendly.

_____ friendly?

3 Make questions.

1 Mut is their dog.
   Is Mut their dog?
2 You are Mickey's sister.
3 He is our new postman.
4 Mut is friendly.
5 They are in their garden.
6 This is London Avenue.
7 You are Millie.

4 a Copy and complete the table with *isn't*, *aren't* or *am*.

Questions	Short answers
Are you our new postman?	Yes, I _____. No, **I'm not**.
Is this London Road?	Yes, it **is**. No, it _____.
Are they in the garden?	Yes, they **are**. No, they _____.

b Give the short answers.

1 Is Millie Mickey's sister? Yes, *she is*.
2 Are Mickey and Millie ten? No, they _____.
3 Are they in the garden? Yes, _____.
4 Is the man their neighbour? No, he _____.
5 Is he their new postman? _____, _____ is.
6 Are you their neighbour? No, I _____.
7 Is Mut your dog? No, he _____.
8 Are you friendly? Yes, I _____.

Listening, speaking and writing

5 a Complete the dialogue.

Mickey	Hello, [1]_____ you our new neighbours?
Stella	Yes, we [2]_____. My [3]_____ Stella and this is [4]_____ brother, David.
Mickey	Pleased to [5]_____ you. [6]_____ Mickey and [7]_____ is my [8]_____, Millie.
Stella	[9]_____ to meet you, too.

b Work with a partner. Make new dialogues.

6 a (1.49) Listen to three new students. What are their names? Choose from these names.

Maria   Connor   Simon   Henry   Dana   Gemma

A Hello. This is Connor. He's your new classmate. He isn't from Oxford.
B Are you from Australia?
C Yes, I am.
D Are you from Sydney?
C No, I'm not.
E Are you from Melbourne?
C Yes, I am.
B How old are you? Are you thirteen?
C No, I'm not.
D Are you twelve?
C Yes, I am.

b (1.49) Listen again. Find this information for each student.

name?   boy / girl?   from?   age?

c Write about the students.

The first student is Connor. He's a boy.
He's from Melbourne in Australia. He's twelve.

d Who are you? Work with three friends. Use the questions:

Are you a man / a woman?
Are you from …?
Are you a singer / a film star / a sportsperson?

Remember you can only ask *Yes* or *No* questions.

2D What day is it today?

Vocabulary

1 a Write the days of the week in the correct order.

Monday

Saturday
Thursday
Monday
Friday
Sunday
Tuesday
Wednesday

Do you know the days of the week in English?

b 🎧 1.50 Listen and repeat.

Is it Tuesday today?

No, it isn't. It's Wednesday.

2 🎧 1.51 Listen. What day do you hear?

Friday

Comprehension

3 a 🎧 1.52 Read and listen. Are the statements true or false?

1 *The Birthday Show* is on Sunday.
2 The song is for Mel's brother.
3 His birthday is on Tuesday.
4 He is thirteen on his birthday.
5 Mel's at home.
6 Joe's at his friend's house.

b Work with a partner. Act the dialogue.

DJ	Hi. It's Saturday. My name's Jez Jones and this is *The Birthday Show*. Hello. What's your name?
Mel	Mel Bradley.
DJ	Hi, Mel. How old are you?
Mel	I'm ten.
DJ	And who is your song for?
Mel	It's for my brother, Joe.
DJ	When's his birthday?
Mel	It's on Tuesday.
DJ	And how old is he?
Mel	He's twelve on Tuesday.
DJ	OK. Where are you? Are you at home?
Mel	No, I'm not. I'm at the shops.
DJ	Is Joe there, too?
Mel	No, he isn't. He's at home.
DJ	Well, happy birthday, Joe, from your sister, Mel. Here's the song.

Grammar

4 Copy and complete the table.

These are yes / no questions

be: questions	
Yes / No	**Wh–**
_____ you at home?	Where **are you**?
Is he thirteen?	How old is _____?

These are wh- questions.

5 a Put the words in the correct order to make questions.

1 you   are   How old
 How old are you?
2 your   name   is   What
3 you   from   are   Where
4 When   your   birthday   is
5 What day   is   today   it
6 is   Where   Joe
7 your   is   brother   How old
8 What   your   phone number   is
9 this   mobile   Whose   is
10 my   Where   books   are

b Match the answers to the questions to make dialogues.

a It's 762954
b It's William, but everyone calls me Billy.
c He's in the garden.
d I'm twelve.
e They're on the table.
f I'm from Spain.
g It's Friday.
h It's Charlotte's.
i He's fifteen.
j It's on Saturday.

c Work with a partner. Read the dialogues.

● *How old are you?*
○ *I'm twelve.*

Listening

6 a 🎧 1.53 Listen to two more dialogues. Answer the questions.

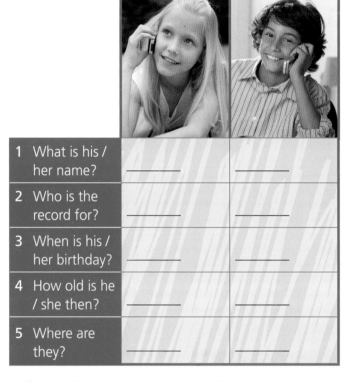

1	What is his / her name?	_____	_____
2	Who is the record for?	_____	_____
3	When is his / her birthday?	_____	_____
4	How old is he / she then?	_____	_____
5	Where are they?	_____	_____

b Work with a partner. Act the dialogues. Use the chart.

c Work with a partner. Make your own dialogues.

Writing

7 a Complete the DJ's text.

> Our caller [1]_____ Mel Bradley. [2]_____ ten. The song is for [3]_____ brother. [4]_____ name's Joe and [5]_____ twelve on Tuesday.

b Write texts for the girl and boy in exercise 6a and you.

What's your address?

1 a Look at the pictures. Do you know anything about these places?

b (🔊 1.54) Read and listen to the texts. Copy and complete the chart.

Address	Where is it?	Why is it famous?
1		
2		
3		
4		

c What famous streets are there in your country? Why are they famous?

This is 10 Downing Street in London. It's the British Prime Minister's home. People often call it just 'Number 10'. It's actually a very big house. There are a hundred rooms in it.

Whose home is this? Not a real person's. But the house is real. It's 221b Baker Street in London, and it's the home of the famous detective, Sherlock Holmes. Today it's a museum about him.

Abbey Road is in London, too. Why is it famous? It's on The Beatles' album 'Abbey Road'. The crossing is outside their recording studio at 3 Abbey Road. There's a webcam there now, so you can see it on your computer.

2 Look at the address. How do you write an address in your country?

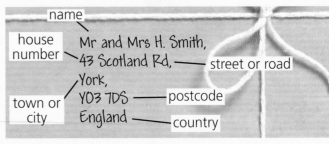

name
house number
Mr and Mrs H. Smith,
43 Scotland Rd, — street or road
York,
town or city
YO3 7DS — postcode
England — country

3 a Complete the short forms of these addresses with these words.

Ave   St   Rd

1 London Road   London _____
2 Victoria Street   Victoria _____
3 Park Avenue   Park _____

b Write these in the short form.

High Street   Sydney Avenue   York Road

4 a (🔊 1.55) Listen. Write the addresses.

1
65 _____

2

b Work with a partner. Ask and answer. Use the addresses in exercise 4a.

● *What's your address?*
○ *It's sixty-five …*

c Work with a partner. Ask and answer about your own addresses.

City of Liverpool
PENNY LANE L18

Penny Lane is also famous because of The Beatles. It's the name of one of their songs. Do you know it? Penny Lane isn't in London. It's in Liverpool. The Beatles were from Liverpool.

English Across the Curriculum

Geography: the world

1 a Look at the map. Match the words with the photos.

desert   mountain   river   ocean

b On the map find the names of:

– a desert   – the four oceans
– four rivers   – three mountain ranges

2 a Look at the map. Change the underlined words.

1 The Indian Ocean is between <u>Europe</u> and Oceania.
The Indian Ocean is between Africa and Oceania.
2 North America and South America are between the Pacific Ocean and the <u>Arctic Ocean</u>.
3 <u>Europe</u> is between the Atlantic Ocean and the Indian Ocean.
4 The Arctic Ocean is next to North America, <u>Antarctica</u> and Asia.
5 Oceania is between the Indian Ocean and the <u>Arctic Ocean</u>.
6 The letter a is in Africa, Antarctica, America, and <u>Europe</u>.

b 🎧 1.56 Listen and check.

3 a 🎧 1.57 Listen. Point to the places you hear.

b 🎧 1.57 Listen again and repeat.

4 Look at the map. Answer the questions.

1 Where's the Nile River?
It's in Africa.
2 Where are the Himalayas?
3 Where's the Sahara Desert?
4 Where are the Rocky Mountains?
5 Where's the Amazon River?
6 Which ocean is next to four continents?
7 Which continent is cold?
8 Which continent is your country in?

ARCTIC OCEAN

NORTH AMERICA
Rocky Mountains   Mississippi
ATLANTIC OCEAN
Amazon
Andes
SOUTH AMERICA

EUROPE
Sahara Desert
Nile
AFRICA

ASIA
Himalayas   Yangtze
INDIAN OCEAN

PACIFIC OCEAN
OCEANIA

ANTARCTICA

Vocabulary

1 Complete the family tree.

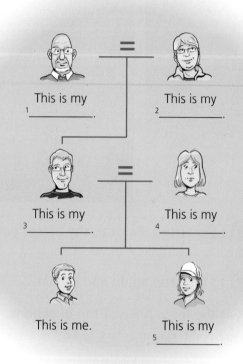

This is my
1 _____.

This is my
2 _____.

This is my
3 _____.

This is my
4 _____.

This is me.

This is my
5 _____.

2 Put the letters in the correct order to make the days of the week.

1 ahdustyr _____
2 uynsad _____
3 astudye _____
4 yrstdaau _____
5 ifadyr _____
6 dedyewsna _____
7 oydamn _____

Short forms

3 Rewrite the sentences. Use short forms.

1 We are in the garden.
2 I am at the shops.
3 Mel is not at home.
4 They are not from the USA.
5 He is our teacher.
6 I am not ten.
7 It is my birthday today.
8 Where is Joe?

Short forms and possessive adjectives

4 Complete the sentences with *his*, *her*, *their*, *he's*, *she's* or *they're*.

1 This card is for my brother. It's _____ birthday today. _____ twelve.
2 There's Mr and Mrs Smith with _____ three dogs. _____ all black.
3 • Where's Andy?
   o _____ in the garden with _____ friends.
4 • Are they Molly's bags?
   o No _____ bags are in the car. _____ Mel's bags.
5 This is Mel's grandmother. _____ from London. Buddy is _____ dog.

Questions with *be*

5 Complete the dialogues with questions.

1 • _____?
   o My name's María Cortéz.
   • _____?
   o I'm from Spain.
   • _____?
   o I'm thirteen.
2 • _____?
   o It's for my brother.
   • _____?
   o Pedro.
   • _____?
   o He's eleven.

Possessive *'s*

6 Use the cues. Write sentences.

1 Mel / pen
   This is Mel's pen.
2 Joe / watch
3 Jack and Susan / dog
4 Buddy / ball
5 Mary / book
6 Granddad and Grandma / house

Planning your project

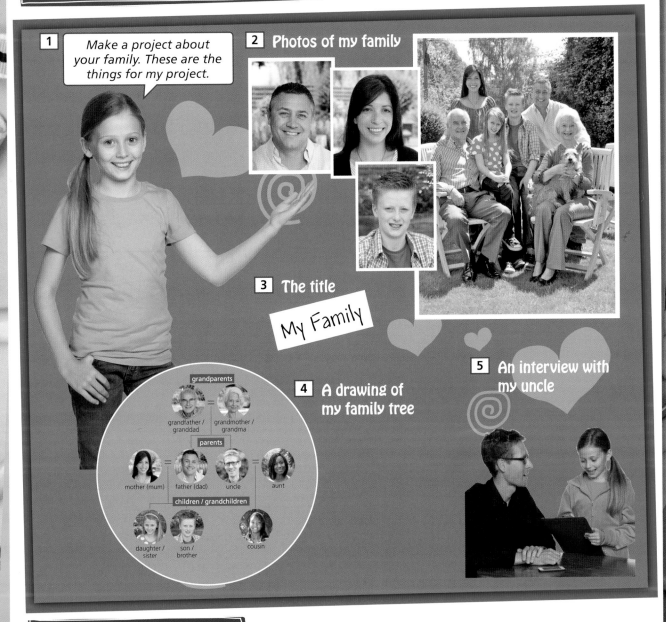

1 Make a project about your family. These are the things for my project.

2 Photos of my family

3 The title

My Family

4 A drawing of my family tree

grandparents

grandfather / granddad — grandmother / grandma

parents

mother (mum) — father (dad) — uncle — aunt

children / grandchildren

daughter / sister — son / brother — cousin

5 An interview with my uncle

Song

1 🎧 1.58 Listen and sing.

My Bonnie

My Bonnie is over the ocean. — Bring back, bring back.
My Bonnie is over the sea. — Oh, bring back my Bonnie to me, to me.
My Bonnie is over the ocean. — Bring back, bring back.
Oh, bring back my Bonnie to me. — Oh, bring back my Bonnie to me.

3 My world

3A I've got a computer

Vocabulary

1 a 🎧 **2.2** Listen and repeat.

1 a games console

2 a television

3 a radio

4 a mobile phone

5 an MP3 player

6 a skateboard

7 a DVD player

8 a bike

9 a camera

10 a remote-controlled car

b 🎧 **2.3** Listen. Which thing do you hear?

Comprehension

2 🎧 **2.4** Read and listen. Answer the questions.

Who has got:
- a computer in his bedroom?
- a computer in the living room?
- a sister to play computer games with?

My friend Tom is lucky. He's got a computer in his bedroom. I haven't got a computer in my room. We've got a computer, but it's for me and my sister. It's in the living room.

I've got a computer in my bedroom.

My friend Joe's lucky. He hasn't got a computer in his room, but he's got a sister to play computer games with. I haven't.

Grammar

3 a Copy and complete the table with the full forms.

have got: affirmative			
I You We They	've	got	a computer. a dog. two cousins. three pens. a watch. two cameras. a car.
He She It	's		

b Complete the sentences with *have got* or *has got*.

1 Tom *has got* a computer.
2 Joe _____ a sister.
3 I _____ two English books.
4 Joe _____ a remote-controlled car.
5 We _____ a good teacher.
6 Mickey _____ a dog.
7 You _____ my pens.
8 They _____ a skateboard.

c Now say the sentences with short forms.

4 a Look at the table.

have got: negative			
I You We They	have **not** haven't	got	an exercise book. a skateboard. a sister. a camera. a dog. a pen. a bike. a brother.
He She It	has **not** hasn't		

How do we make have got *and* has got *negative?*

b Use the table. Make three sentences about yourself and three about your friend.

5 Make true sentences. Use the cues.

She hasn't got a bag. She's got a box.

1 a bag / a box   2 a car / bikes

3 a mobile / a camera   4 a dog / a cat

5 a remote-controlled   6 an apple / an orange
car / a skateboard

Listening

6 a 🎧 2.5 Look at the things in exercise 1. Listen. Tick (✓) the things Ravi has got.

b Say what Ravi has and hasn't got.

He's got a …   He hasn't got a …

Speaking

7 Work in a group. Play a game.

I've got a book.
He's got a book and I've got a mobile.
He's got a book. She's got a mobile and I've got a bag.

Comprehension

1 a 🔊 2.6 **Read and listen. Choose the correct presents and match them to the names.**

Mickey
Millie
Mut

- a blue bag
- a new blanket
- a red jumper
- a new cricket bat
- a big bone
- a yellow ball

b Who are the presents from?

2 Work in a group. Act the story.

Vocabulary

3 a 🎧 2.7 **Listen and repeat.**

These words are adjectives. They describe things.

Colours
yellow   **green**   orange

red   **black**   brown

blue   white   grey

Others
big small   **thick** THIN

old **new**   GOOD bad

l o n g short

b Find something in your classroom for each adjective.

This exercise book is red.

Grammar

4 a Look at the story. Rewrite the sentences with the words *red* or *good*.

I've got a jumper.
They've got presents.
We've got two presents for our birthday.

Where do we put the adjective?

b Rewrite the sentences. Put the words in brackets in the correct order.

1 I've got _____ (a present big).
   I've got a big present.
2 She's got _____ (books thick four).
3 We've got _____ (teacher a good).
4 Where's _____ (jumper yellow my)?
5 I've got _____ (cats two black).

Speaking and writing

5 a Work with a partner. Look at the pictures.
Student A: cover one picture.
Student B: cover the other picture. Now ask and answer. Use the cues.

1 a skateboard
A *Mickey's got a red skateboard in my picture. Is it red in your picture, too?*
B *No, it isn't. He's got a green skateboard in my picture.*

2 a T-shirt	6 a book
3 a bag	7 a mobile
4 a watch	8 a cap
5 a pencil	9 a radio

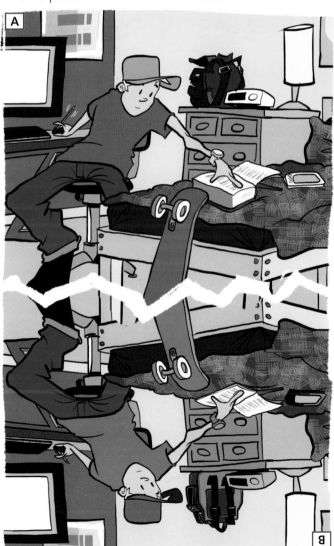

b Now write about the differences.

Mickey's got an orange cap in picture A, but he's got a blue cap in picture B.

Vocabulary

1 a 🎧 2.8 **Listen and repeat.**

1 a hamster

2 a rabbit

3 a rat

4 a snake

5 a horse

6 a mouse

7 a fish (plural: fish)

8 a spider

9 a budgie (a bird)

10 a parrot (a bird)

b 🎧 2.9 **Listen. What kind of animal is it?**

This is a small animal. It's got a long, thin tail. The one in the picture is grey.

Comprehension

2 a 🎧 2.10 **Listen and match the people to the pets.**

	a rabbit
Joe	a cat
Mel	a spider
	a snake

b **What colour are the pets?**

Teacher	Have you got a dog or a cat, Joe?
Joe	No, I haven't, Miss. I've got a snake.
Teacher	Really? Is it a big snake?
Joe	No it isn't, but it's beautiful. It's red and white.
Teacher	Has your sister, Mel, got a pet, too?
Joe	Yes, she has.
Teacher	What's she got?
Joe	She's got a rabbit.
Teacher	That's nice. What colour is it?
Joe	Grey. It's boring. It's always asleep!

Grammar

3 **Copy and complete the table.**

have got: questions and short answers

You have got a pet.	
_____ _____ a pet?	Yes, I have. No, I haven't.
He has got a pet.	
_____ _____ a pet?	Yes, he has. No, he hasn't.

How do we make questions with have got *and* has got?

4 Make questions.

1 You've got a pet.
   Have you got a pet?
2 She's got a brother.
3 They've got a car.
4 He's got a bike.
5 You've got a computer.
6 Our neighbours have got a dog.
7 Mel's got an MP3 player.
8 Joe's got a mobile.

5 Look at the picture and make sentences. Use the cues.

1 Anita / a spider
   Anita's got a spider.
2 Fai and Bao / a parrot
   Fai and Bao haven't got a parrot.
   They've got a hamster.
3 Amy / horse
4 Steve / two dogs
5 Karel and Anna / two mice
6 Lulwah and Fahad / a cat
7 Ed / five fish
8 Jose and Maria / three rabbits
9 Ali / a hamster
10 Carlotta / three birds

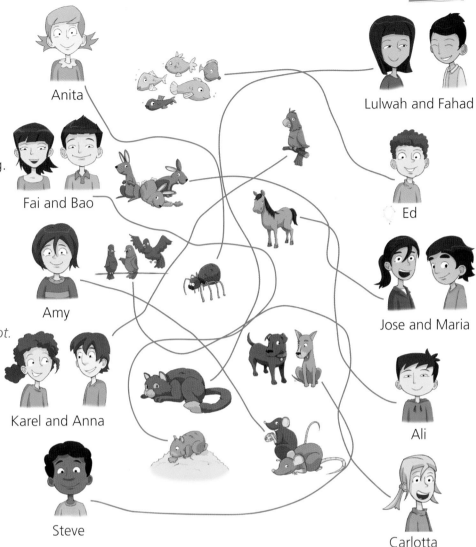

Anita

Lulwah and Fahad

Fai and Bao

Ed

Amy

Jose and Maria

Karel and Anna

Ali

Steve

Carlotta

6 Work with a partner. Ask and answer. Use the cues in exercise 5.

• *Has Anita got a spider?*
◦ *Yes, she has.*
• *Have Fai and Bao got a parrot?*
◦ *No, they haven't. They've got a hamster.*

Listening

7 🎧 2.11 Listen and complete the chart.

		pet	name	colour
1	Ollie			
2	Phoebe			
3	Salim			
4	Alice			

Speaking

8 Work with a partner. Ask and answer questions.

1 a pet
   Have you got a pet?
   Yes, I have. / No, I haven't.
2 a brother   6 a bike
3 a sister   7 an MP3 player
4 a favourite band   8 a computer
5 a radio

9 Work in a group. Play a game.

A *What have I got in my bag beginning with P?*
B *Have you got a pencil?*
A *No, I haven't.*
C *Have you got a pen?*
A *Yes, I have.*

Vocabulary

1 a 🎧 2.12 Look at the pictures. Listen and repeat.

b Which of these subjects have you got in your timetable? What are your favourite subjects? Which subjects are you good at?

1 Art and Design

2 English

3 French

4 Geography

5 History

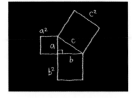

6 Maths

7 ICT (Information and Communication Technology)

8 RE (Religious Education)

9 PE (Physical Education)

10 Music

— Science —

11 Physics

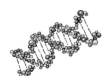

12 Biology

13 Chemistry

14 Design and Technology

15 Citizenship

Comprehension

2 Look at Joe's timetable and the text with the photos. Answer the questions.

1 What class is Joe in?
2 What lessons has he got on Wednesday?
3 Has he got lessons on Saturday?
4 What are PE, RE and ICT?
5 When has he got a double lesson of Maths?
6 How many students are there in his class?
7 Which science has he got this term?

Name: Joe Bradley			Class: 8C	
Monday	Tuesday	Wednesday	Thursday	Friday
8.30–9.00 Registration and assembly				
9.00–10.00	French	English	Maths	French	Geography
10.05–11.05		Citizenship	ICT	PE	Art
11.05–11.20 Break				
11.20–12.20	Maths	Technology	Music	History	RE
12.20–1.20 Lunch				
1.20–2.20	Science	PE	English	Maths	Science
2.25–3.25					

This is our Maths class with our Maths teacher, Mr Woods. He's very nice, but I'm not very good at Maths. My favourite subject is Science.

Tuesday afternoon is great. We've got double PE.

We've got four lessons of Science a week. We do one science each term. This term it's Physics, last term it was Chemistry and next term it's Biology.

This is my school. I'm in year 8. There are thirty students in my class. We wear a uniform. It's blue and black.

Speaking and listening

3 Compare your school to Joe's. Answer the questions.

1 What class are you in?
2 How many students are there in your class?
3 Do you wear a uniform?
4 Have you got the same subjects as Joe?
5 What is your favourite day? Why?
6 Do you have registration and assembly in the morning?
7 When is your lunch?
8 Have you got lessons on Saturday?

4 Work with a partner. Ask and answer. Use the cues.

1 English / Wednesday
   • *Has Joe got English on Wednesday?*
   ○ *Yes, he has.*
   • *Have we got English on Wednesday?*
   ○ *No, we haven't.*
2 PE / Tuesday
3 History / Monday
4 Art / Friday
5 ICT / Thursday
6 Science / Monday
7 Music / Friday
8 PE / Thursday
9 Maths / Tuesday
10 Geography / Wednesday

5 (2.13) Look at Joe's timetable in exercise 2. Listen. What day is it?

Schools in England and Wales

1 🎧 2.14 **Read and listen to the information about schools in England and Wales. Look at the chart and answer the questions.**

1 How old are pupils in:
   Year 1?   Year 6?   Year 9?
2 How many years are they at primary school?
3 How many years are they in the sixth form?
4 Are pupils at school on Saturday?
5 Where do pupils have lunch?

The school day is from about 8.45 to about 3.30.
There are no lessons on Saturday and Sunday, but
a lot of secondary schools have got sports matches
on Saturday morning.
Most pupils have their lunch at school.
About half have a school lunch and half bring
sandwiches from home (a packed lunch).
Most schools have got a school uniform.

2 **Compare the information to your country. Make a chart of the school system in your country.**

3 🎧 2.15 **Listen and find this information for each person.**

1 What class is he / she in?
2 What are his / her favourite subjects?
3 What colour is his / her school uniform?
4 Does he / she have a school lunch?

1 Sasha   2 Henry   3 Rob   4 Noelie

Year	Age	School		
1	5–6	primary	compulsory	
2	6–7	primary	compulsory	
3	7–8	primary	compulsory	
4	8–9	primary	compulsory	
5	9–10	primary	compulsory	
6	10–11	primary	compulsory	
7	11–12	secondary	compulsory	
8	12–13	secondary	compulsory	
9	13–14	secondary	compulsory	
10	14–15	secondary	compulsory	
11	15–16	secondary	compulsory	
12	16–17	secondary		sixth form
13	17–18	secondary		sixth form

break

a packed lunch

English Across the Curriculum

Science: we are animals, too

1 a 🎧 2.16 Listen. Match the words to numbers 1–9.

mouth
hand
body
arm
head
foot
eye
leg
nose

b 🎧 2.17 Listen. Touch or point to the part of the body you hear.

arm

2 a 🎧 2.18 Listen and label the picture.

| fur   a beak   feathers   legs   a tail |
| teeth   whiskers   a wing |

b 🎧 2.19 Listen. If it's part of a bird, say 'tweet tweet'. If it's part of a cat, say 'miaow'.

 fur   *miaow*

3 Test your partner. Use words from exercises 1 and 2 and these expressions. Ask and answer.

- *Have cats got …?*
- *Have birds got …?*
- *Have humans got …?*

○ *Yes, they have. / No, they haven't.*
○ *Yes, they have. / No, they haven't.*

- *Have birds got wings?*
- *Have humans got a tail?*

○ *Yes, they have.*
○ *No, they haven't.*

4 Work with a partner. Play a game.
  A Pick an animal from here or page 32.
  B Ask Yes / No questions to find the animal.

- *Has it got four legs?*
- *Has it got a tail?*

○ *Yes, it has.*
○ *No, it hasn't.*

5 Here are four dogs: Fido, Woof, Rover and Shep. Read the sentences. Which dog is which?

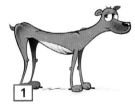

1 Rover hasn't got long legs.
2 Woof hasn't got large ears.
3 Shep and Fido have got short tails.
4 The dog with a short body isn't Woof.
5 Fido has got small eyes.

Vocabulary

1 Write down six of each of these things.

1 colours   3 adjectives
2 school subjects   4 possessions

2 Find eight animals.

d	f	c	b	h	o	r	s	e	j
f	g	s	i	o	k	a	w	v	m
v	u	p	o	r	a	b	b	i	t
t	j	i	p	d	h	w	s	q	n
b	s	d	h	k	e	v	n	r	m
i	o	e	g	u	k	l	a	d	o
r	c	r	b	n	h	r	k	l	u
d	s	o	u	o	e	p	e	f	s
h	a	m	s	t	e	r	s	e	e
p	a	r	r	o	t	c	h	n	r

have got / has got

3 Make true sentences. Use *'ve / 's got* or *haven't / hasn't got*.

1 I _____ a dog.
2 We _____ Science on Wednesday.
3 Our school _____ a uniform.
4 I _____ a skateboard.
5 We _____ English today.
6 My best friend _____ a pet.
7 Our English teacher _____ short hair.
8 I _____ blue eyes.

4 a Put the words in the correct order.

1 on got we have Maths Tuesday?
2 Joe a got sister? has
3 has legs how many got? a spider
4 crocodile got a has feathers?
5 has bike? got our teacher a
6 you have bag? got a red
7 have we today? got what subjects
8 a got have pet? you

b Use your questions. Ask and answer with a partner.

Listening

5 a 🎧 2.20 Listen. Complete the chart. Tick (✓) the things Edward and Martha have got.

	Edward	Martha
a games console		
a television		
a radio		
a mobile phone	✓	
a remote-controlled car		
a skateboard		
a DVD player		
a bike		
a camera		
a pet		
a brother		

b Write six true sentences about Edward and Martha. Use *has / hasn't got*.

Your Project

Working together

Make a project about your school. Here's our project.

Miss Jones

This is our Biology teacher, Miss Jones. She's married, but hasn't got any children.

Mr Walker

This is Mr Walker. He's our maths teacher. He's 36. He's married and he's got two children.

Our School

timetable

school system

teachers

uniform

activities

Miss Jones

Mr Walker

Song

1 Complete the song. The words are all on page 34.

2 (🎧 2.21) Listen and check. Then listen and sing.

My favourite day

Chorus
Hey! Hey! It's OK
It's our favourite day today.

We haven't got ¹E _ _ _ _ _ h, we haven't got ²F _ _ _ _ h,
We haven't got ³A _ t or ⁴H _ _ _ _ _ y.
We haven't got ⁵M _ _ _ s, we haven't got Games,
We haven't got ⁶M _ _ _ c or ⁷G _ _ _ _ _ _ _ y.

Chorus

We haven't got ⁸R _, we haven't got Science,
We haven't got ⁹B _ _ _ _ _ y or ¹⁰I _ T.
We haven't got ¹¹P _ _ _ _ _ s, we haven't got ¹²P _,
We haven't got ¹³b _ _ _ k or ¹⁴a _ _ _ _ _ _ y.

Chorus
So what's today? Well, it isn't ¹⁵M _ _ _ _ y,
¹⁶T _ _ _ _ _ y, ¹⁷W _ _ _ _ _ _ _ y, ¹⁸T _ _ _ _ _ _ y
or ¹⁹F _ _ _ _ y.
What's today? It's our favourite day. No school today.
It's Saturday!

4A What's the time, please?

Vocabulary

1 🎧 2.22 **Look at the clocks. Listen and repeat.**

ten to six

five to nine

five o'clock

five past three

ten past seven

quarter to one

quarter past eight

twenty to four

twenty-five to twelve

half past ten

twenty-five past eleven

twenty past two

to past

2 a Write the times. Use these words.

| quarter past   ten to   twenty to   five past   quarter to   half past   twenty-five to   o'clock |

1 *It's quarter past four*

2 *It's...*_____

3 _____

4 _____

5 _____

6 _____

7 _____

8 _____

b Rewrite this with the correct punctuation.

whatsthetimepleaseitssevenoclock

3 🎧 2.23 **Listen. Write the times you hear.**

1 twenty to four

Comprehension

4 Read the conversation and answer the questions.

1 When is the party?
2 Why can't Molly go to the party?

Mrs Dawson	When is Ravi's birthday party?
Molly	It's on Saturday.
Mrs Dawson	What time?
Molly	It's at four o'clock. Why?
Mrs Dawson	Well, you've got a piano exam at half past four on Saturday.
Molly	Oh no!

Grammar

5 Copy and complete the table.

> When do we use on and at?

on, at

The party is _____ Saturday.
It's _____ four o'clock.
You've got a piano exam _____ half past four _____ Saturday.

Listening, speaking and writing

6 a Look at the chart. Work with a partner. Ask and answer. Point to a clock.

- *What's the time, please?*
- *It's quarter to four.*

b 🎧 2.24 **Listen to the dialogues. Match the activities to the days and times.**

Activity	Day	Time
the volleyball match	Monday	
Annie's dance lesson	Tuesday	
the school concert	Wednesday	
Jim's piano exam	Thursday	
the hockey game	Friday	
Fred's party	Saturday	
Claire's tennis lesson	Sunday	

7 Work with a partner. Look at the chart in exercise 6. Ask and answer.

- *When is the volleyball match?*
- *It's on Friday at eight o'clock.*

8 Write the days and the times.

The volleyball match is on Friday at eight o'clock.

Vocabulary

1 🎧 2.25 **Listen and repeat the expressions in blue.**

Comprehension

2 🎧 2.26 **Read and listen to Molly's day. Put the things in the correct order.**

bus dinner homework lunch
book breakfast TV shower
teeth bed

I get up at half past seven and I have a shower.

At ten to eight I have breakfast in the kitchen and I listen to the radio.

Then I brush my teeth and put on my coat.

At quarter past eight I go to school with my friends. We take the bus.

Lessons start at quarter to nine.

We have lunch at school at half past twelve. I have a packed lunch.

We finish school at half past three and go home.

I do my homework and go on the Internet before dinner.

We have dinner at six o'clock.

After dinner I watch TV or listen to music.

I go to bed at half past nine. I read a book or a magazine for half an hour and then I go to sleep.

Grammar

3 a Look at the grammar table.

Present simple	*This is the present simple tense.*
I **get up** at seven o'clock. We **take** the bus to school. Lessons **start** at quarter to nine.	

b Complete the sentences.

1 I *have* breakfast in the kitchen.
2 My mum and dad _____ to work at half past eight.
3 I _____ books and magazines in bed.
4 At the weekend, I _____ up at half past nine.
5 Lessons _____ at half past three.
6 I _____ the bus to school with my friends.
7 I _____ my homework from seven o'clock to eight o'clock.

c Write seven sentences about your day.

4 a 🎧 2.27 **Read and listen.**

I go to school from
Monday to Friday.

I don't go to school on
Saturday and Sunday.

b Copy and complete the table with the short form.

How do we make the present simple tense negative?

Present simple: negative		
I You We They	**do not** _____	get up at eight o'clock. take the train to school. have lunch at home. finish school at three.

5 a Complete the sentences with the negative form of the words in brackets.

1 I *don't get up* at seven o'clock. (get up)
2 I _____ TV when I have breakfast. (watch)
3 My friends and I _____ to school. (walk)
4 You _____ home for lunch. (go)
5 Lessons _____ at three o'clock. (finish)
6 We _____ dinner at half past five. (have)
7 I _____ my homework with my friends. (do)
8 We _____ computer games. (play)
9 They _____ to school on Saturdays. (go)
10 I _____ music in bed. (listen to)

b Make sentences about yourself.

I get up at seven o'clock. / I don't get up at seven o'clock.

Listening and writing

6 🎧 2.28 **Listen. Molly's school has an Internet exchange with a school in China. She's talking about a typical day for the children there. Are these statements true or false?**

1 The children arrive at school at twenty past seven.
2 They all take the school bus.
3 Morning lessons are from 8 to 12 o'clock.
4 All children have a packed lunch at school.
5 They have two hours for lunch.
6 Afternoon classes finish at quarter to four.
7 The children do their homework at school.
8 They go to bed at quarter past eight.

7 a Write six sentences about a typical day in your life. Four are true and two are false.

b Read your sentences to a partner. He / She must find the false ones.

4C Free time

Vocabulary

1 a (🎧 2.29) **Listen and repeat.**

1 play football

2 play tennis

3 play ice hockey

4 play computer games

5 play the piano

6 play the guitar

7 play the violin

8 collect badges

9 go skiing

10 go swimming

11 go to dance class

12 watch DVDs

b (🎧 2.30) **Listen. Which activity do you hear?**

1 play tennis

Comprehension

2 (🎧 2.31) **Read and listen to Molly. Find three pictures for each person.**

A B C
D E F
G H I

1

Molly

I like sport. I play tennis with my friends, and I watch tennis on TV. I like music, too. I play the piano, and I also go to dance school. We've got classes on Wednesdays and Saturdays. I don't play computer games.

2

Kirk

My brother, Kirk, likes sport. He plays football. He has training after school on Tuesdays. He goes swimming with his friends at the sports centre, too. He doesn't play a musical instrument, but he collects football cards. He's got 200!

3

Eddie

Our neighbour, Eddie, doesn't like sport. He doesn't play tennis or football and he doesn't go swimming. He doesn't play a musical instrument and he doesn't collect football cards. In his free time, Eddie watches DVDs, reads comics and plays computer games.

Grammar

3 a Copy and complete the table.

What happens after he and she?

Present simple: endings	
I **play** football.	She _____ tennis.
We **have** piano lessons.	He _____ training.
They **watch** TV.	He _____ DVDs.
I **go** swimming.	She _____ to dance school.

b Match the subjects and the verbs.

play / like

I   you   we   they   he   she   it

plays / likes

c Look at your answers to exercise 2. What do the people do?

Molly plays tennis. She … .

4 Look at Molly's day on page 42 again. Write about it.

Molly gets up at half past seven and she has a shower.

5 a Copy and complete the table. Find the missing words in the text in exercise 2.

Present simple: negative
I _____ play computer games.
He _____ play a musical instrument.

b Complete what Molly says. Use *don't* or *doesn't*.

1 I _____ get up at six o'clock.
2 Eddie _____ collect football cards.
3 We _____ play ice hockey at our school.
4 Kirk _____ play the piano.
5 Eddie _____ like sport.
6 Kirk and Eddie _____ go to dance class.
7 I _____ play football.

6 (2.32) **Listen. Say the negative.**

I play tennis.
I don't play tennis.

Speaking, listening and writing

7 Work in a group. Play a game.

She doesn't like sport and I don't like Maths.

I don't like sport.

8 a (2.33) **Listen. What do the people do? Tick the correct pictures.**

1 Juraj *Slovakia*		1 Guang *Thailand*	
	✓		
	✗		

b Write about the people in exercise 8a.

Juraj plays ice hockey. He doesn't play football.

9 What do you do in your free time? Write a paragraph. Use these phrases.

I like …, I …, and I …, I don't like …, and I don't … .

4D Mickey, Millie and Mut

Comprehension

1 a Read the story. Answer the questions.

1 Who is Millie talking to?
2 Where do Mickey and Millie play tennis?
3 Why doesn't Mut go with them?

b 🎧 2.34 Read and listen.

1 Mickey and Millie's uncle and aunt are visiting them from Australia.

Do you like sport, Millie?

Yes, I do, Uncle Bob.

What sports do you play?

I play … volleyball, table tennis. I go swimming, too, but my favourite sport is tennis.

2 Does Mickey play tennis, too?

Yes, he does. We play every Saturday.

3 Oh, where do you play? Do you go to the sports centre?

No, we don't. We go to the park.

TENNIS COURTS

5 Oh, why not?

Because he always catches the ball.

4 Does Mut go with you?

No, he doesn't.

2 Are the statements true or false, or doesn't it say?

1 The man is Mickey and Millie's grandfather.
2 Millie doesn't like sport.
3 She plays tennis.
4 She doesn't go swimming.
5 Mickey doesn't like volleyball.
6 Mickey and Millie go to the park every Saturday.
7 They play tennis there at ten o'clock.
8 They don't take Mut to the park.
9 Mut catches their tennis balls.

Grammar

3 a Copy and complete the table with *do* and *does*.

How do we make questions in the present simple?

Present simple: questions and short answers

		play volleyball?	Yes, I _____.
_____	you	go swimming? collect things?	No, I **don't**.
_____	he	like sport? watch TV?	Yes, he _____. No, he **doesn't**.

b Complete the questions with *Do* or *Does*.

1 _____ you collect badges?
2 _____ Eddie go skiing?
3 _____ Molly play tennis?
4 _____ Molly and her friends play football?
5 _____ you go swimming?
6 _____ Kirk play a musical instrument?

c Work with a partner. Make dialogues. Use the questions in exercise 3b.

• *Do you collect badges?*
◦ *Yes, I do or No, I don't.*

4 Copy and complete the table. Put the words in brackets in the correct order.

Present simple: *wh-* questions

Where _____ tennis? (play you do)	
When _____ to school? (she does go)	

5 Work with a partner. Use the cues. Ask and answer.

1 When / Molly have breakfast
   When does Molly have breakfast?
   She has breakfast at ten to eight.
2 When / you go to school
3 Where / Molly have lunch
4 When / we go home
5 Where / you do your homework
6 When / Mickey and Millie play tennis

Speaking and writing

6 a Look at the chart. Do you do these things? Write ✓ or ✗ for Me.

	Me	My partner
play the		
get up at		
listen to the ___ in the morning		
take the ___ to school		
play		
go		
collect		
write a lot of		

b Work with a partner. Ask and answer. Write ✓ or ✗ for My partner.

• *Do you play the piano?*
◦ *Yes, I do or No, I don't.*

c Write about yourself and your partner.

I don't play the piano. My partner plays …

Sport

1 a (2.35) **Read and listen to the information. Copy the chart and write the names of the sports in columns 1 and 2.**

1 Britain	2 The USA	3 My country

These are popular sports in Britain:
football   rugby   cricket   snooker

These are popular sports in the USA and Canada:
American football   baseball   basketball
ice hockey

Tennis and golf are also popular in all these
countries.

b **What sports are popular in your country? Complete column 3.**

2 (2.36) **Read the text. Copy and complete the chart.**

	Girls	Boys
winter	*hockey*	
summer		

In British schools, pupils normally have a
double lesson of PE each week.

In most schools, boys play football or rugby in
the winter. In summer, they play cricket and
they do athletics.

Girls normally play hockey or netball (a kind
of basketball) in the winter. They play tennis
and they do athletics in the summer.

Most schools have a sports day in the summer.
There are races and other athletics events, like
the high jump, long jump and javelin. Parents
and grandparents come to
watch, and there are prizes
for the winners.

3 **How often do you have PE in your school? What things do you do? Do you have a sports day?**

4 a (2.37) **Listen. What sports do Cherry and Marcus play? Which ones do they like?**

Cherry   Marcus

b (2.37) **Listen again. Answer the questions.**

1 What school teams are they in?
2 What sports do they watch on television?
3 Why does Cherry like sports day?
4 Why doesn't Marcus like cricket?

English Across the Curriculum

Music: musical instruments

1 (2.38) **Read and listen.**

There are lots of different kinds of musical instruments.

a trumpet
This is a wind instrument.

a guitar
This is a string instrument.

a xylophone
This is a percussion instrument.

2 a **Copy the chart and write the instruments in the correct column.**

Wind instrument	String instrument	Percussion instrument
a trumpet	a guitar	a xylophone

b (2.39) **Listen and check.**

a harp

a piano

a trombone

a tambourine

a clarinet

drums

a violin

a saxophone

a flute

a double bass

an electric guitar

a keyboard

a harmonica

3 (2.40) **Listen. What instruments do you hear?**

4 **Do you play a musical instrument? What are your favourite instruments?**

5 **Work with a partner. Mime playing a musical instrument. Ask questions about the instrument.**

- *Is it a clarinet?*
- *No, it isn't.*
- *Is it a saxophone?*
- *Yes, it is.*

Present simple: affirmative and negative

1 a **Complete the sentences with the correct form of the verbs.**

| work ~~have got~~ do go play watch go |

1 Mike *has got* two brothers and a sister.
2 We _____ basketball at school.
3 Sarah _____ skiing in France.
4 We _____ in a shop.
5 Mr West _____ to work by car.
6 My parents _____ TV in the evening.
7 Mandy _____ her homework in the kitchen.

b **Make the sentences negative.**

Present simple: questions

2 Make questions.

1 You're from Australia.
   Are you from Australia?
2 It's my turn.
3 We have lunch at one o'clock.
4 They like football.
5 I'm in this photo.
6 Peter takes the bus to school.
7 Mr and Mrs Johnson have got a new computer.
8 Jane finishes school at quarter past three.

Vocabulary

3 Look at the picture clues. Complete the words or phrases. What is phrase 9?

Listening, writing and speaking

4 a (2.41) **Listen and complete the chart about Kenton.**

Name	
From	
Age	
Phone number	
Brothers and sisters	
School	
Favourite subjects	
Free time	
Musical instrument	

b **Now complete the text. Use the information from exercise 4a.**

Kenton [1]_____ comes from [2]_____. He's [3]_____ years old. His phone number's [4]_____ He [5]_____ a brother, but he [6]_____ a sister. His name's [7]_____. Kenton [8]_____ to [9]_____ High School. His favourite subjects are [10]_____ and [11]_____. In his free time he [12]_____, and he [13]_____ and [14]_____. He [15]_____ a musical instrument.

c **Write a text about yourself.**

d **Interview your partner. Use the chart in exercise 4a.**

What's your name?
It's …

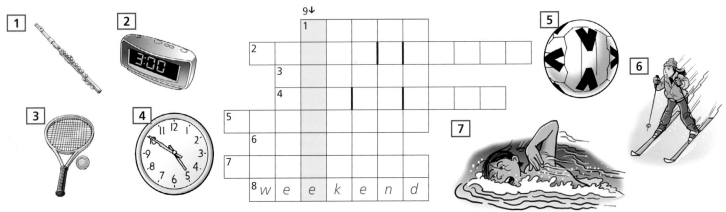

9↓

2								
3								
4								
5								
6								
7								
8 w	e	e	k	e	n	d		

Your Project

4

Helping each other

1 Make a project about your free time. Write about:
- your favourite hobby
- the hobby of someone that you know (a friend or another family member.)

Add photos to your project.

2 We help each other with our projects:

3 Interviews

What do you do in your free time, John?

4 Taking photos

5 Checking

My friend, John, go cycling.

It isn't, 'go'... It's, 'He goes'...

Oh yes. Thank you.

6 Commenting

This is great. I like this photo. Do you go to dance class every week?

Song

1 a Read and guess the missing words.

Digital Charlie

Chorus
Charlie ¹_____ play
Any sport at all.
Football, tennis, ²_____,
Golf or volleyball.
He just plays ³_____ games.
At that he is a winner.
Then he watches ⁴_____
Till it's time for dinner.

I collect stamps and cards
And play a lot of ⁵_____.
Mirabelle ⁶_____ magazines
And books of any sort.
Benjamin ⁷_____ cycling
Until his face is red.
But Charlie ⁸_____ DVDs
Until it's time for ⁹_____.
Chorus

We are all at ¹⁰_____ all week,
But when the weekend comes,
Martha ¹¹_____ the xylophone
And Maxwell plays the ¹²_____.
Wilma goes to dance class
On ¹³_____ and Sunday.
But Charlie's on the Internet
From Friday night till ¹⁴_____.
Chorus

b 🎧 2.42 **Listen and check.**

5A My room

Vocabulary

1 a (2.43) **Look at the picture. Listen and repeat the words.**

9 a poster
12 a mirror
4 a lamp
10 a chest of drawers
5 a desk
1 a bookshelf
2 a bedside table
11 a wardrobe
3 a bed
7 a chair
6 a rug
8 a carpet

b (2.44) **Listen. Complete the sentences with the correct places.**

The remote-controlled car is on …   the chair.

Comprehension

2 a (2.45) **Look at Ravi's room. Read and listen. Who is Robby?**

This is my room. I've got a bed, a wardrobe and a chest of drawers. There's a desk, too. It's in front of the window. I do my homework there. I've got posters of my favourite bands and sports stars on the wall. You can see some of my things in the picture, too. My skateboard's in the wardrobe and my guitar's on the bed. And that's Robby, my robot, on the rug next to the bed. He's great!

b Find eight things in the picture that Ravi doesn't mention.

the clock

Grammar

3 a (2.46) **Listen and repeat.**

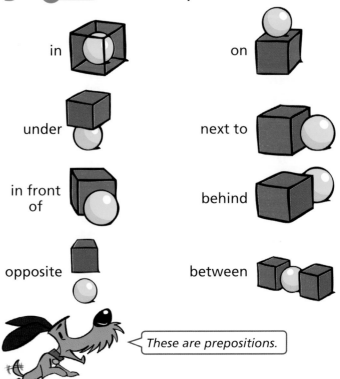

in

on

under

next to

in front of

behind

opposite

between

These are prepositions.

b Look at the pictures. Where's Robby?

He's on the bookshelf.

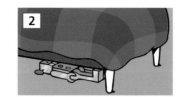

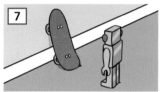

4 a Look at the picture of Ravi's room on page 52. Work with a partner. Describe the position of the things. Use the cues.

1 the football / on
   The football is on the chest of drawers.
2 the chair / in front of
3 the bedside table / between
4 the lamp / behind
5 the rug / next to
6 the bag / under
7 the bookshelf / opposite
8 the skateboard / in
9 the football boots / in front of
10 the clock / on

b Work with a partner. Ask and answer about the things.

- *Where's the football?*
- *It's on the chest of drawers.*

Listening, writing and speaking

5 a ⏵ 2.47 **Listen. Where are the things? Connect the things to the places 1–7.**

> book   mobile phone   pen   CD
> umbrella   watch   bag

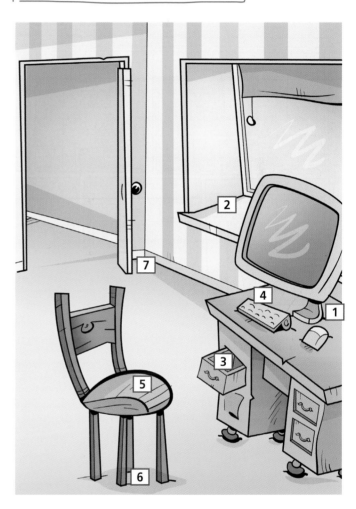

b Write a sentence about each thing.

The pen is next to the computer.

6 Work with a partner. Play a game.
A Choose something in the classroom.
B Ask *Yes / No* questions to find it.

B   Is it in front of me?
A   No, it isn't.
B   OK. So it's behind me. Is it on the wall?
A   Yes, it is.
B   Is it next to the window?
A   Yes, it is.
B   It's the map of the world.
A   Correct.

Comprehension

1 (🎧 2.48) **Look at the picture. Read and listen. Which of the places in blue is not in the picture?**

This is our house.

Upstairs there are three bedrooms – my bedroom, my sister, Vama's bedroom and our parents'. There's a bathroom upstairs, too.

Downstairs there's a hall, a living room, a dining room and a kitchen. There isn't a cellar under my house. The dining room is next to the kitchen. There's also a toilet under the stairs.

In this picture, I'm in the living room. Vama is in her bedroom, and our parents are in the kitchen. Our dog, Jack, is in the hall.

Outside there's a garden and we've got a garage for our car, too.

2 a **Read the text again. Label the parts of the house.**

1 upstairs

b (🎧 2.49) **Listen, check and repeat.**

3 (🎧 2.50) **Listen. Which room is Ravi in?**

He's in the bedroom.

Grammar

4 **Copy and complete the table.**

We use There is and There are … to describe places.

There is / are + room		(+ part of house)
There _____	a bathroom	upstairs.
There _____	three bedrooms.	
There _____	a cellar.	
There **aren't**	two bathrooms.	

5 **Look at the picture of Ravi's house again. Complete the sentences.**

1 *There's* a television in the l_____ r_____.
2 _____ four rooms u_____.
3 _____ a bathroom d_____.
4 _____ four b_____.
5 _____ a toilet under the s_____.
6 _____ two people in the k_____.
7 _____ a dog in the h_____.
8 _____ a TV in the d_____.
9 _____ a car in the g_____.
10 _____ two bikes in the g_____.

Vocabulary

6 a (2.51) **Look at the pictures. Listen and repeat.**

1 an armchair
2 curtains
3 a sofa
4 a light

5 a fridge
6 a cooker
7 a cupboard
8 a sink

9 a shower
10 a washbasin
11 a toilet
12 a bath

b Which things 1–12 can you see in Ravi's house. Where are they?

There's a cooker and a sink in the kitchen.

c What other things can you see in Ravi's house?

There are wardrobes in the bedrooms.

Reading and speaking

7 a Copy the plan of a flat. Read the text and label the rooms.

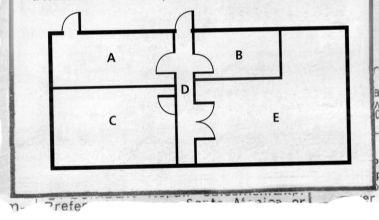

Answering Service Experienced

FLAT TO LET

There are four rooms in the flat and a hall. The hall is room D. There's a small table in the hall. There's a telephone on the table.

Room E is the living room. There's a sofa here and there are two armchairs, too. The television is here. There's a desk here, too, with a chair. There's a computer on the desk.

Room B is the bathroom. There isn't a bath here, but there's a big shower. There's a toilet and a washbasin, too.

There's a big mirror on the wall.

Room A is the kitchen. There are lots of cupboards here. There's a fridge, a sink and a cooker. There's also a television and a radio here. We eat here, so there's a small table and there are four chairs. Room C is the bedroom. There are two beds here. There's a big wardrobe, and a chest of drawers. There's a lamp on the chest of drawers and a clock.

b Read the text again. Draw and label the things in each room.

8 a Add six more things to the flat. Don't show your partner.

b Describe the position of each thing to your partner. He / She must draw it on his / her plan.

In the hall there's a picture on the wall.
There's a rug in the bedroom. It's between the two beds.

9 Describe one of the rooms in your house.

5C Our town

Vocabulary

1 a 🔊 **2.52** **Listen and repeat.**

1 a station

2 a theatre

3 a hospital

4 a church

5 a hotel

6 a bank

7 a cinema

8 a sports centre

9 a swimming pool

10 a café

11 a post office

12 a museum

13 a shopping centre

14 a supermarket

15 a square

b **Which of the places are there near your home?**

There isn't a station near my home.
There are three cafés in my street.

Comprehension

2 🔊 **2.53** **Some people are asking Ravi about places in his town. Read and listen. Answer the questions.**

1 What is the name of Ravi's town?
2 Which of the places in exercise 1 does Ravi mention?
3 Which of the places are in the town?

1 **Boy** Excuse me. Is there a café near here?
Ravi Yes, there's a good one in the park over there.
Girl Thanks.

2 **Man** Is there a cinema in Tunbridge Wells?
Ravi No, there isn't. Well, there isn't one in the town centre. The old cinema is closed now.
Man OK. Thanks.

3 **Woman** Are there two theatres in Tunbridge Wells?
Ravi Yes, there are – The Assembly Hall and The Trinity. The Trinity is over there in Church Road.
Woman Thank you.

Grammar

3 Copy the table. Complete the questions and short answers.

How do we make questions with There is and There are?

There is – questions and short answers

There's a café near here. _____ _____ a café near here?	Yes, **there** _____. No, _____ **isn't.**
There are two theatres. _____ _____ two theatres?	Yes, **there** _____. No, _____ **aren't.**

4 Work with a partner. Use the cues. Make dialogues.

- *Excuse me. Is there a swimming pool here?*
- *Yes, there is. It's at the sports centre.*
- *Thank you.*

1 a swimming pool		Yes / at the sports centre
2 three supermarkets		No / only two
3 a bus station		No / but a big train station
4 a lot of banks		Yes / in the town centre
5 a hospital		No / old hospital closed now
6 a park		Yes / we play tennis there
7 a lot of cafés		Yes / favourite café is in the park
8 two post offices		No / only one in Victoria Road

Listening, speaking and reading

5 a 🎧 2.54 Listen. Connect the places to the prepositions and locations.

1	a post office	in	a	STATION
2	a hotel	next to	b	MUSEUM
3	a bank	behind	c	VICTORIA ROAD
4	a café	in	d	SPORTS SHOP
5	a bus stop	opposite	e	MARKET SQUARE
6	a park	in front of	f	TOWN HALL

b Say where the places are.

The post office is in Victoria Road.

6 a Read the conversation. Do you like Ravi's dream town?

Molly Is there a school in your dream town?
Ravi No, there isn't.
Molly Oh, but … Is there a shop?
Ravi Yes, there are seven sports shops and seven sweet shops.
Molly Why seven?
Ravi One for each day of the week.
Molly I see, and how many cafés are there?
Ravi There are fourteen cafés.
Molly Fourteen? Why? There are only seven days in a week.
Ravi One for the morning and one for the afternoon!

b Plan your own dream town. Choose eight of the places in exercise 1. You can have more than one of each thing.

c Work with a partner. Ask and answer about your dream towns. Use these expressions.

Is there a …?
How many …. are there?

5D Mickey, Millie and Mut

Comprehension

1 🎧 (2.55) **Read and listen. What can Supermut do? What can't he do?**

Mut's Dream

Grammar

2 Look at the table. Make six true sentences about you.

can / can't		
I		fly.
He		speak English.
She		play a musical instrument.
It	**can**	ski.
We	**can't**	ride a bike.
You		swim.
They		run like the wind.

3 Copy the table. Complete the questions and short answers from the story.

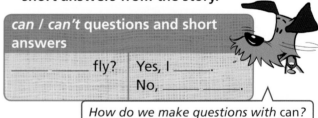

can / can't questions and short answers	
_____ _____ fly?	Yes, I _____. No, _____ _____.

How do we make questions with can?

4 a How well do you know your partner? Write six sentences about him / her with can / can't.

She can play the piano.
She can't …

b Check your ideas. Ask and answer with your partner.

● *Can you play the piano?*
○ *Yes, I can. / No, I can't.*

Mickey, Millie and Mut's day out

5 a 🎧 2.56 **Read and listen.**

b Work in a group. Play a game.

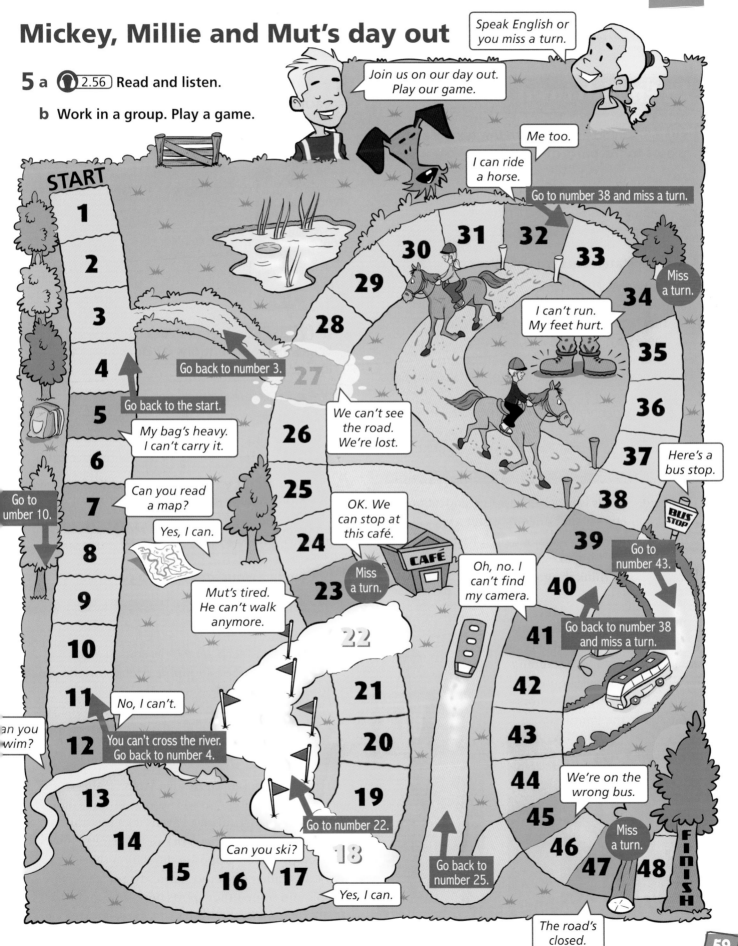

An English town

1 🎧 **2.57** **Read and listen to the text. Match the places to the parts of the town.**

A
The Pantiles
Calverley Grounds
the Precinct

B
the shopping centre
a market
an ice rink

2 **Are the statements true or false?**

1 Tunbridge Wells is in London.
2 It's famous for its old castle.
3 The Pantiles is the old part of the town.
4 There's a post office in the Precinct.
5 Tunbridge Wells hasn't got a museum.
6 You can take a train to the coast from Tunbridge Wells.
7 A lot of people from Tunbridge Wells work in London.
8 You can go swimming in Calverley Grounds.

3 a 🎧 **2.58** **Listen. Write ✓ or ✗ in the chart for each person.**

	lives there	likes it
Jane		
Ivan		
Mark		
Alice		

b 🎧 **2.58** **Look at the cues. Listen again. Which person mentions it? Does he / she like it?**

the sports centre   the cinema   the Pantiles
trains   shops   cafés   the park   theatres
the swimming pool

4 a **Think about your town (or the nearest town to you). Answer the questions.**

1 What do you like about the town?
2 What don't you like?

b **Compare your ideas with a partner.**

Tunbridge Wells is in south-east England, about sixty kilometres from London. It isn't a very old town. It's about 350 years old. So it hasn't got a castle or anything like that. It's famous for its water. People think it's good for you.

This is the old part of the town. It's called the Pantiles. There are lots of cafés and restaurants here. There's a market on Saturdays, too. A lot of visitors come to see the Pantiles.

This is the modern part of the town. People call it the Precinct. The shopping centre and the post office are here. The Town Hall and the police station are here, too. There are also two theatres, a small museum and a library in this part of town.

There's a station in Tunbridge Wells. Trains from here go to London and to Hastings on the coast. A lot of people in Tunbridge Wells take the train to London every day. They work in the banks, offices and shops there. Opposite the station there's a big park. It's called Calverley Grounds. You can play tennis and some other sports here, and there's a nice café, too. In the winter there's an ice rink here and you can go ice skating.

English Across the Curriculum

History: towns and cities

1 **Read the text. What is it about?**

Think about your town or city (or a big town near you, if you live in a village). Why is it there?

1 Is it near a river? Towns are often near rivers or lakes, because water is very important. We need it for drinking and for washing. You can travel by boat on water, too. A lot of big cities, such as Budapest, London and Prague, are near a river.

2 But a river can be a problem if you can't cross it. A lot of towns are in places where there is a bridge (or a ford), so that you can cross the river. You can see this in the names of some British towns, such as Cambridge (a bridge over the river Cam) and Oxford (a place where you can cross the river with your cows). Are there similar names in your country?

3 A lot of towns are on a small hill. Why? A hill is a good place to be because it's safe from floods. And it isn't easy for people to attack you, because you can see them. This isn't important today, but a lot of very old towns are on hills. These towns often have a castle.

4 A lot of old towns are at a crossroads – a place where two roads cross. This is important, because people can come to your town from other places to buy and sell things. These towns often have a big square in the town centre for a market.

2 a **Which of these things does the text mention? Tick them.**

farms   hills   bridges   factories
crossroads   rivers   the sea   stations

b **Why is each of the things that you ticked important?**

3 **Label the numbered things in the pictures.**

4 **Think about your town (or a big town near you). Answer the questions.**

1 Is it an old town?
2 Is it near a river? What is the river called?
3 Are there any bridges in your town?
4 Is the town on a hill?
5 Has it got a castle?
6 Is your town at a crossroads? Where do the roads go to?
7 Has your town got a big square? Is there a market there?
8 Is there another reason why your town is there?

Prepositions

1 **Look at the picture and complete the sentences.**

1 The table is _____ the sofa.
2 The cat is _____ the armchair.
3 The school bag is _____ the sofa and the table.
4 The lamp is _____ the sofa.
5 Ollie is _____ the sofa
6 The sofa is _____ the TV.
7 Ollie's sister is _____ the sofa.

Vocabulary and writing

2 a **Match the words to the places in the picture:**

☐ a station	☐ a shop
☐ a supermarket	☐ a hotel
☐ a cinema	☐ a café
☐ a post office	☐ a church
☐ a square	☐ a swimming pool
☐ a bank	☐ a sports centre

b **Write six sentences about the picture. Use these words.**

There's There isn't There are	in opposite next to behind between in front of

1 *There's a bank opposite the post office.*

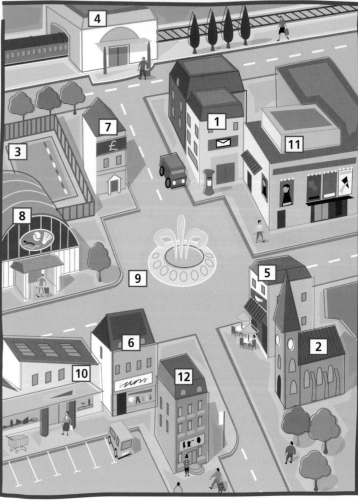

Listening, writing and speaking

3 a (🔊 2.59) **Listen. What can Ben do? Tick (✓) what he can do and cross (✗) what he can't do.**

1 play the piano ☐
2 speak English ☐
3 draw with his left hand ☐
4 swim ☐
5 speak German ☐
6 draw ☐

b **Write six sentences about what Ben can and can't do.**

c **Now ask your partner what he / she can and can't do. Write four sentences.**

Your Project

Getting information

Make a project about your town.

I need these things:
- a map of the town
- leaflets about things to do and see
- photos of some important places
- interviews with some people in the town centre

Where can I get them?
- on the Internet
- from:
  - the tourist information centre
  - the town hall
  - I can take some photos
  - I can talk to people in the town

Song

1 Complete the song. Choose from these words.

opposite	behind	can't	park	front
village	factory	museum	police	can
town	road	bookshop	next	

2 🎧 2.60 Listen and check.

Our town

There's a supermarket next to the ¹_____,
And the church is ²_____ to the clothes shop.
In ³_____ of the doctor's there's a bus stop.
Welcome to our town.

Chorus
Our town, our town. Come and walk around.
Our town, our town. Come and walk around.
Our town, our town. Come and walk around.
Oh we love our town.

Take a look at the map and you ⁴_____ see
There's a ⁵_____ and a school and a library,
A hotel, a bank and a ⁶_____ .
Welcome to our town.

In the middle of the ⁷_____ is the bus station.
⁸_____ the café there's a fire station.
Next to the shops is the ⁹_____ station.
Welcome to our town.

6A My friends

Vocabulary

1 a 🎧 3.2 **Listen and repeat.**

 1 tall

 2 short

 3 fat

 4 slim

 5 long hair

 6 short hair

 7 bald

 8 dark hair

 9 fair hair

 10 brown eyes

  11 blue eyes

12 green eyes

  13 glasses

 14 a moustache

 15 a beard

b 🎧 3.3 **Listen. Write the numbers of the correct pictures to match the descriptions.**

1 *This woman has got brown eyes and dark hair.*

8 …

Comprehension

2 Read the texts. Complete the sentences with the correct names.

1 _____ is short.
2 _____ is very slim.
3 _____ have got short hair.
4 _____ have got blue eyes.
5 _____ has got fair hair.
6 _____ is very tall.

Hi. I'm Carla. I'm tall and I'm very slim. I've got long, fair hair and blue eyes.

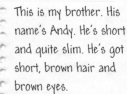
This is my brother. His name's Andy. He's short and quite slim. He's got short, brown hair and brown eyes.

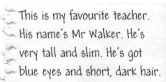
This is my favourite teacher. His name's Mr Walker. He's very tall and slim. He's got blue eyes and short, dark hair.

Grammar

3 Look at the table. Make three sentences from each table.

Describing people: *be* + adjective		
I	'm 'm not	tall. short. fat. slim. bald.
He She	's isn't	

Describing people: *have / has got* + (adjective) + noun			
I	've haven't	got	long hair. dark hair. blue eyes. brown eyes. a beard. glasses.
He She	's hasn't		

We often use these words in descriptions.

very He's **very** slim.
She isn't **very** tall.

quite He's **quite** fat.

4 a Match the words to the people.

| brown hair   brown eyes   a moustache   long hair |
| short   slim   green eyes   fair hair   short hair |
| tall   blue eyes   black hair   fat   bald |

b Describe the people.

1 She isn't very tall. She's got short black hair and brown eyes.

Speaking and listening

5 Work with a partner.
A Look through the book and choose a person. Don't show your partner.
B Ask questions about the person to find out who it is.

A   OK. This person is a man.
B   Is he tall?
A   No, he isn't.
B   Is he slim?
A   Yes, he is.
B   Has he got fair hair?
A   No, he hasn't. He's bald.
B   Has he got a moustache or a beard?
A   Yes, he has. He's got a beard.
B   Is it the teacher on page 81?
A   Yes, it is.

6 a (3.4) Listen and draw the people.

b Work with a partner. Compare your pictures.

Hello. My name's Frank N. Stein. I've got a very strange family.

Writing

7 a Work in a group. Make your own strange family. Draw some people or cut pictures from magazines or comics.

b Write a description of each person.

Comprehension

1 a Look at the pictures. Find the people.

Carla   Billy   Andy   Mrs Fletcher

b 🎧 3.5 Read and listen. Answer the questions.

1 Why is Billy at home?
2 Why are Carla and Andy in the car?
3 Why are Carla and Andy buying pens and balloons?

1 It's ten o'clock on Saturday morning. Carla is getting in the car with her brother Andy. They're going into town.

2 *Ring, ring*

Their friend, Billy, isn't going into town. He's at home, because he's ill. He's lying in bed.

3 *Hi, Billy. We're in the car.*

Are you going to the sports centre?

4 *No, we aren't. We're going into town. Are you watching TV?*

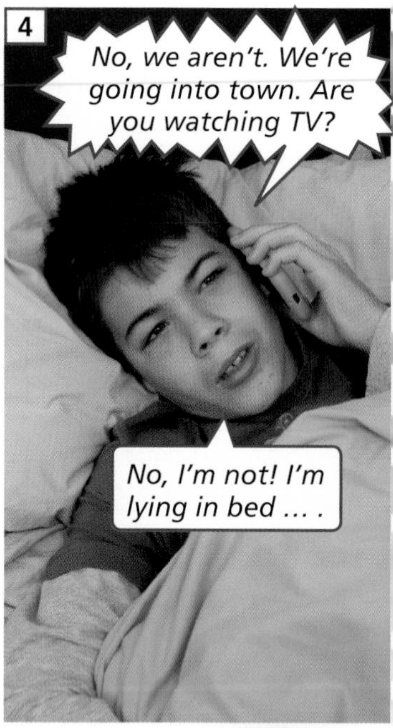

No, I'm not! I'm lying in bed ... .

5 We're in the department store now. Andy's buying some balloons. I'm not buying balloons. I'm looking for some pens. Ah, here they are.

6 *What are you doing?*

We're making a poster.

It's one o'clock. They aren't shopping now. They're at home

7 *Hi, Billy. Are you in bed?*

Hi, Carla. No I'm not in bed now. I'm watching TV in the living room

8 *Well, look out of your window.*

Get Well Soon Billy

2 Complete the sentences with the names of the people.

Picture 1: _____ are getting in the car.
Picture 2: _____ is lying in bed.
Picture 3: _____ are sitting in the car.
Picture 4: _____ is talking to Carla.

Picture 5: _____ is buying some pens.
Picture 6: _____ are making a poster.
Picture 7: _____ is watching TV.
Picture 8: _____ is looking out of the window.

Grammar

3 a **Copy and complete the table with 's, 'm, 're.**

We use the present continuous tense to say what is happening now.

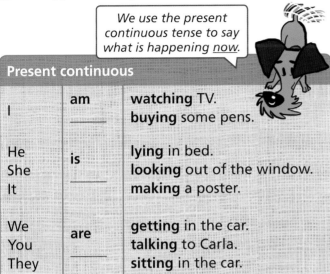

Present continuous		
I	am _____	**watching** TV. **buying** some pens.
He She It	is _____	**lying** in bed. **looking** out of the window. **making** a poster.
We You They	are _____	**getting** in the car. **talking** to Carla. **sitting** in the car.

b **Work in pairs. Student A chooses a picture from the story. Student B says what's happening.**

A *Picture 6*
B *Carla and Andy are making a poster*

4 **It's quarter to eight on Monday morning. Complete the sentences with the present continuous of the verbs in brackets.**

1 Carla*'s having* a shower. (have)
2 Andy _____ his teeth. (brush)
3 Their parents _____ the radio. (listen to)
4 Mr Fletcher _____ a cup of coffee. (make)
5 Mrs Fletcher _____ the newspaper. (read)
6 Joe and Mel _____ their books in their bags. (put)

5 a **Find the negative of these sentences in the story in exercise 1.**

Present continuous: negative
I'm buying balloons. _____ balloons. Billy's going into town. _____ into town. They're shopping now. _____ now.

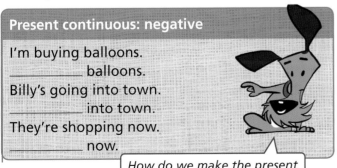

How do we make the present continuous negative?

b **It's now quarter past eight. Make sentences. Use the cues and your answers to exercise 4.**

1 Carla / wait for the bus
Carla isn't having a shower now. She's waiting for the bus.
2 Andy / phone Billy
3 Their parents / go to work
4 Mr Fletcher / walk to the station
5 Mrs Fletcher / have breakfast
6 Joe and Mel / get in the car

Listening and speaking

6 🎧 **3.6** **Listen. What is Carla doing?**

She's going swimming.

7 a 🎧 **3.7** **Listen. Complete the dialogue.**

- *Can I ¹_____ you?*
- *How ²_____ is this pen?*
- *It's 75p.*
- *And how much are ³_____ balloons?*
- *⁴_____ 50p each.*
- *⁵_____ I have a pen and five balloons, please?*
- *That's £3.25 then, ⁶_____.*
- *Here ⁷_____ are.*
- *Thank ⁸_____.*

b **Make new dialogues to buy the things.**

Comprehension

1 a 🎧 3.8 **Read and listen. Answer the questions**

1 Why are Mickey and Millie washing Mut?
2 Why does Millie say: 'Well done!'?

b Work in a group. Act the story.

1 It's Saturday morning. We go to the park every Saturday morning.

Come on, Mut!

2 We aren't going to the park today. I'm having a bath! Huh!

3 Is it raining?

No, it isn't. It's sunny today.

I play in the garden when it's sunny, but I'm not playing in the garden at the moment. Millie's brushing my fur.

4 What are Mickey and Millie wearing?

They usually wear jeans and sweatshirt. at the weekend, but they're wearing smar clothes now.

5 Come on, Mut. We're going out now.

Are we going to the shops? We go to the shops every Saturday afternoon.

6 Are we going in the car, Dad?

Yes, we are.

We usually go into town on the bus, but we're going in the car today. And we aren't going to the, shops. Where are we going?

7

8 And the winner of the first prize is ... Mut!

Well done, Mut!

You're the best!

2 Complete the sentences with the words.

park	smart	fur	washing
bus	winner	raining	show

1 They aren't going to the _____ today.
2 Mickey and Millie are _____ Mut.
3 It isn't _____ this morning, but Mut isn't playing in the garden.
4 Millie is brushing Mut's _____.
5 Mickey and Millie are wearing _____ clothes.
6 They aren't taking the _____ into town.
7 They're going to a pet _____.
8 Mut is the _____.

Grammar

3 Copy the table. Complete the questions and short answers.

How do we make questions in the present continuous?

Present continuous: questions and short answers	
We're going in the car. _____ _____ _____ in the car?	Yes, we _____. No, we **aren't**.
It's raining. _____ _____ _____ ?	Yes, it **is**. No, it _____.

4 a Make questions and short answers. Use the cues.

1 they / go to the park / No
Are they going to the park? No, they aren't.
2 Mut / have a bath / Yes
3 it / rain / No
4 Mickey and Millie / go to the shops / No
5 Mickey / brush Mut's fur / No
6 Mickey and Millie / wear smart clothes / Yes
7 they / go in the car / Yes

b Work with a partner. Practise your dialogues.

5 Copy and complete the table.

We use the present simple with every day, all the time and usually. We use the present continuous with now, today and at the moment.

Present simple
We **go** to the park every Saturday morning. I **play** in the garden when it's sunny. They **wear** jeans and sweatshirts at the weekend.

Present continuous
We **aren't going** to the park today. I _____ **playing** in the garden at the moment. They _____ smart clothes now.

6 Complete the sentences with the correct tense of the words in brackets.

1 I *am listening* to music at the moment. I *listen* to music every day. (listen)
2 Carla _____ jeans every weekend. She _____ jeans now. (wear)
3 We _____ the car today. We _____ the car every Sunday. (wash)
4 Carla and Andy _____ to the shops every Saturday. They _____ to the shops now. (go)
5 Carla _____ tennis today. She _____ tennis on Tuesdays and Fridays. (play)

Speaking and listening

7 Work with a partner. Mime an activity. Ask questions about the activity.

A   Are you playing a computer game?
B   No, I'm not.
A   Are you texting?
B   Yes, I am.

8 a 🎧 3.9 Copy the chart. Listen. It's six o'clock on Wednesday. What are the people doing at the moment? Complete column 1. Use these verbs.

cook   practise   do   go swimming   watch

	now	every day?
Carla		
Billy		
Carla's dad		
Carla's mum		
Andy		

b 🎧 3.9 Do the people do the activities every day? Listen again. Write *Y* or *N* in column 2.

6D Clothes

Vocabulary

1 a 🎧 3.10 **Listen and repeat.**

4 a sweatshirt
7 a coat
10 a tie
14 a cap
12 a jacket
11 a shirt
1 a jumper
2 a skirt
5 jeans
8 a dress
13 trousers
15 shorts
3 boots
9 shoes
6 socks
16 trainers

A   B   C   D   E

b 🎧 3.11 **Close your book. Listen. Which person is wearing the things? Say A, B, C, D or E.**

This person's wearing a black jacket   D

2 What are you and your friends wearing now?

I'm wearing a blue shirt, black jeans, …
Elsa's wearing …

Comprehension

3 a Read the dialogue. How much does Carla pay?

b 🎧 3.12 **Listen and check.**

Grammar

4 Copy and complete the table.

How much is / are …?		
How much _____ _____ T-shirt?		
_____ £8.50		
How much _____ _____ jeans?		
_____ £17.20.		

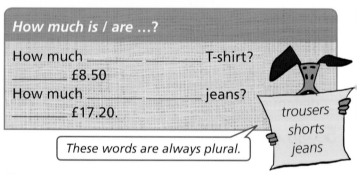

These words are always plural.

trousers
shorts
jeans

5 Work with a partner. Make shopping dialogues about these clothes.

1	a jumper: €35		4	shorts: €20.60
2	trousers: £59		5	socks: $8
3	a cap: $7		6	a sweatshirt: £26

Carla	How much is this T-shirt, please?
Assistant	It's £8.50.
Carla	What about this sweatshirt?
Assistant	That's £25.
Carla	Oh. And how much are these jeans?
Assistant	They're £17.20.
Carla	Can I have the jeans and the T-shirt then, please?
Assistant	OK. That's £ _____, please.

Reading and speaking

6 a Look at the pictures and answer the questions.

1 What is happening in each picture?
2 What is the king wearing in Picture A?

b Read the story. Put the pictures in the correct order.

c 🔊 3.13 Listen and check.

It's Saturday, and the Royal Show is starting. The king is on his white horse. The people are in the street. They know about the king's clothes.

I can't see the clothes, but I don't want to look stupid.

Look at the people. They're singing and shouting. They can all see my beautiful new clothes.

One day two men come to the royal palace. They say they are tailors and they want to show the king their clothes.

We've got some beautiful clothes for the king. They're magic clothes.

Only clever people can see these clothes. Stupid people can't see anything.

Why are you laughing?

Look at the king. He isn't wearing any clothes!

Your Majesty, look at this red jacket ... this white shirt ... these black trousers ... and these blue shoes.

Are they holding any clothes? I can't see them, but I don't want to look stupid.

Oh, they're beautiful! I can wear them for the Royal Show on Saturday.

It's true I'm not wearing any clothes. I really am stupid!

Why is everyone laughing at me? Are they all stupid?

Ha ha ha! The king isn't wearing any clothes!

In a country far away lives a king. He loves clothes.

Look at the king. He's wearing a beautiful gold coat.

He's wearing a big red hat, too. He always wears beautiful clothes.

7 Work in a group. Act the story of the king's new clothes.

71

People

1 **a** (3.14) Read and listen to the information. Where were all these people born?

b Copy and complete the chart.

Name	Lives in	The family is from	Speaks
Gabi	*Edinburgh*		

2 Find the names of six English-speaking countries in the texts.

3 Look at the map on pages 82 and 83 and find the countries.

4 Answer the questions.

1 Are there people from other countries in your country? Where are they from?
2 Do many people from your country live abroad? Which countries do they usually go to?

People from all over the world live in Britain. These young people were all born in Britain, but their parents or grandparents are from other countries.

1 Gabi lives in Edinburgh in Scotland. Her grandfather is from Hungary. 'We usually go to Budapest every summer, but I don't speak Hungarian. It's a very difficult language. Luckily, all my cousins there learn English at school.'

2 Mei's family is from Singapore. They live in Birmingham. Her parents work in a hospital there. 'I speak English and Chinese,' says Mei. 'We always speak Chinese at home, but at school I only speak English. Some of my friends are Chinese, too, but we always speak English to each other.'

3 Desmond's grandparents are from Nigeria in Africa. Desmond lives in Manchester. 'Everyone in Nigeria speaks English. It's the national language,' he says. 'There are a lot of African languages there, too, but I don't speak any of them. I only speak English. I'm learning French at school.'

4 Kathir lives in Oxford. His parents are from Sri Lanka. 'We speak English at home,' he says. 'My parents also speak Tamil – an Indian language – but I don't. I can speak Spanish. We learn it at school and it's my favourite subject.'

5 This is Emre. His family is from Turkey. 'There are a lot of Turkish people in our part of London, so I speak English and Turkish. I speak English most of the time, but we visit my grandparents in Turkey every year and they don't speak English.'

People from Britain live and work in other countries, too. Most of them go to other English-speaking countries – Australia, New Zealand, South Africa, Canada and the USA. A lot of people from Britain now live and work in other European countries, too.

Art: describing people

1 a Read the text. Choose the correct answers.

This painting shows people in a park on Sunday afternoon. The park is on an island called *La Grande Jatte*. It's in the River Seine in Paris. In the picture we can see a river, people, trees, boats and animals, but look closely. It's really just dots of colour.

The painter is Georges Seurat. He painted it in 1884.

1 Where is the park in the painting?
   a Berlin   b London   c Paris
2 Who is the painter?
   a Picasso   b Seurat   c Whistler
3 When was it painted?
   a 1884   b 1910   d 1840

b What can you see when you look at the picture closely?

2 a How many of these things can you see in the painting?

boats   umbrellas   dogs   children

b How many people are:

- holding an umbrella?   - fishing?
- not wearing a hat?   - rowing?
- running?   - playing a musical
- lying on the grass?   instrument?

c What animal is the woman in the black hat holding?

3 🔊 3.15 Listen. Find the people in the painting.

This person is sitting on the grass next to the river. Her friend is standing in front of her. She's fishing.

4 Do you like the painting? Why? Why not?

Present continuous

1 a Look at the pictures. What are Dominic and Mark doing? Ask and answer with a partner.

Dominic   Mark

b 🎧 **3.16** Listen. Are the pictures correct?

1 *No. They aren't playing football. They're playing tennis.*

Present simple or present continuous?

2 Complete the sentences with the correct tense of the verbs in brackets.

1 We *get up* late on Sundays. (get up)
2 ● Come on, Vicky. It's quarter past eight.
   ○ OK. I _____ now. (get up)
3 ● Is Jess in the garden?
   ○ Yes, she _____ with Tess. (play)
4 Tony _____ swimming every Saturday. (go)
5 Bye, Mum. We _____ to the cinema. (go)
6 ● What are you doing?
   ○ I _____ to The Wanted on my MP3 player. (listen)

Speaking

3 Complete the dialogue. Practise it with a partner.

- ¹_____ I _____ you?
- ○ How ²_____ is _____ pen?
- ³_____ £5.25.
- ○ And ⁴_____ much _____ these badges?
- They're £1.14.
- ○ Can I ⁵_____ the pen and a badge ⁶_____?
- ⁷_____ £6.39 altogether.
- ○ ⁸_____ you are.
- Thank you. That's 61p ⁹_____.
- ○ Thank ¹⁰_____.

Describing people

4 a Describe the people. Write three sentences about each person.

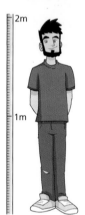
James

Alex

Beth

1 James is *tall and slim*.
   He's got _____.
   He's wearing _____.
2 Alex is _____.
   He _____.
   _____.
3 Beth is _____.
   She _____.
   _____.

b Now write three true sentences about yourself.

Presenting and sharing your project

1 Make a project about people. They can be:
- photos of people that you know
- pictures of famous people
- pictures from magazines.

Write about the people in your pictures.
- What do they look like?
- What are they wearing?
- What are they doing?

2 What do you do with your projects?

3 We put our projects on the classroom wall.

4 We post our projects on the OUP website.

5 Our projects are on the wall in the corridor.

6 We upload our projects onto the school website.

7 We email our projects to a school in England.

This is my best friend, Ailsa. She's quite tall and slim. She's got long, fair hair and green eyes. She's wearing a pink top, grey trousers and a red cycle helmet. In this photo she's sitting on her bike. She's looking at her brother, Donald. He's cycling. David is wearing a red cycle helmet, too. He's also wearing a blue sweatshirt and blue jeans and white trainers. David is quite tall and slim, too. He's got short brown hair and grey eyes.

Song

1 Complete the song with the correct form of the verbs: eat go wear

b 🎧 3.17 Listen and check.

Red pyjamas

I ¹_____ red pyjamas today.
I ²_____ red pyjamas today.
I ³_____ them as a rule,
But I'm really late for school.
So I ⁴_____ red pyjamas today.

Peter ⁵_____ a banana today.
Yes, he ⁶_____ a banana today.
He ⁷_____ them all the time
And they keep him feeling fine
Peter ⁸_____ a banana today.

We ⁹_____ to the shops today.
Yes, we ¹⁰_____ to the shops today.
We ¹¹_____ there every Sunday
And we sometimes stay till Monday.
Yes, we ¹²_____ to the shops today.

Land on a word

Take turns to throw the dice. Write down the words you land on. Make a sentence with your words. The first person to make a correct sentence with at least four words is the winner. If you make a wrong sentence, you miss a turn.

START

lives does we where
do isn't
in the
when under
breakfast drink
how play
playing doesn't
is here
what there
Saturday don't
like aren't
he you
why she
reading opposite
are every day
quarter I
to

Phonetic symbols

Consonants

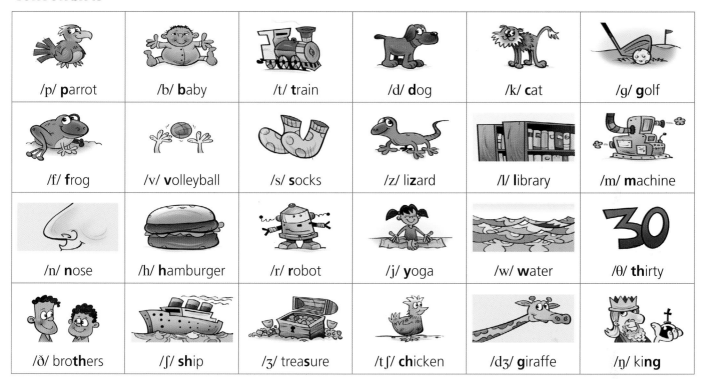

/p/ **p**arrot	/b/ **b**aby	/t/ **t**rain	/d/ **d**og	/k/ **c**at	/g/ **g**olf
/f/ **f**rog	/v/ **v**olleyball	/s/ **s**ocks	/z/ li**z**ard	/l/ **l**ibrary	/m/ **m**achine
/n/ **n**ose	/h/ **h**amburger	/r/ **r**obot	/j/ **y**oga	/w/ **w**ater	/θ/ **th**irty
/ð/ bro**th**ers	/ʃ/ **sh**ip	/ʒ/ trea**s**ure	/tʃ/ **ch**icken	/dʒ/ **g**iraffe	/ŋ/ ki**ng**

Vowels

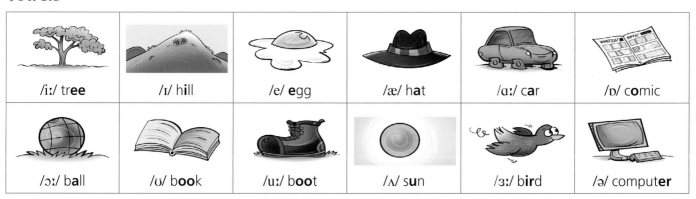

/iː/ tr**ee**	/ɪ/ h**i**ll	/e/ **e**gg	/æ/ h**a**t	/ɑː/ c**a**r	/ɒ/ c**o**mic
/ɔː/ b**a**ll	/ʊ/ b**oo**k	/uː/ b**oo**t	/ʌ/ s**u**n	/ɜː/ b**i**rd	/ə/ comput**er**

Diphthongs

/eɪ/ pl**a**ne	/əʊ/ p**o**ster	/aɪ/ b**i**ke	/aʊ/ h**ou**se
/ɔɪ/ t**oy**	/ɪə/ **ea**r	/eə/ h**ai**r	/ʊə/ t**ou**rist

Pronunciation

Unit 1

Sounds and letters

1 🎧 **3.18** **Listen and repeat the words.**

same letter	different sound
man	/mæn/
watch	/wɒtʃ/
name	/neɪm/

different letter	same sound
door	/dɔː/
your	/jɔː/
board	/bɔːrd/

2 a 🎧 **3.19** **Listen to the pairs of words. If the sounds are the same, clap your hands.**

o			a	
1 open	close	5	bag	watch
2 dog	boy	6	glass	are
3 forty	box	7	apple	stand
4 two	phone	8	name	draw

b 🎧 **3.19** **Listen again and repeat the words.**

A rhyme

3 a 🎧 **3.20** **Listen and say the rhyme.**

One, two, three, four, five.
Once I caught a fish alive.
Six, seven, eight, nine, ten.
Then I let him go again.
Why did you let him go?
Because he bit my finger so.
Which finger did he bite?
This little finger on my right.

b Find all the words with the letter 'i'. Which ones have the same vowel sound as 'fish' and 'five'?

A tongue twister

4 **How fast can you say this?**

Oranges, pictures, glasses and watches,
Toothbrushes, pencils, apples and boxes.

Unit 2

/ə/ endings

1 🎧 **3.21** **A lot of words in English have an /ə/ sound in the last syllable. Listen and repeat.**

father   brother   America   woman
garden   Britain   cousin   sister

2 Can you find your way across the river? You can only step on stones with the /ə/ sound in the last syllable.

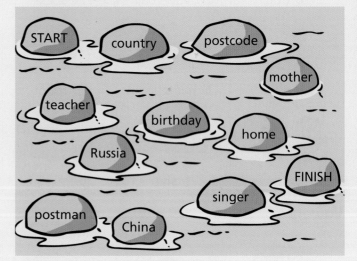

A rhyme

3 a 🎧 **3.22** **Listen and say the rhyme.**

Tinker, tailor, soldier, sailor,
Rich man, poor man, beggar man, thief.
Doctor, lawyer, Indian chief.

b 🎧 **3.22** **Listen to the first line of the rhyme again. How do we pronounce the second syllable of each word?**

A tongue twister

4 How fast can you say this?

Granddad, father, uncle, brother.
Grandma, sister, aunt and mother.

Unit 3

Short and long vowels

1 a (🎧 3.23) **Listen and repeat.**

Short vowels		Long vowels	
/ɪ/	fish	big	/iː/	green	he
/e/	ten	pet	/ɑː/	car	France
/æ/	cat	man	/ɔː/	horse	door
/ɒ/	box	got	/uː/	blue	you
/ʌ/	number	lucky	/ɜː/	bird	world
/ʊ/	look	good			

b Give one more word for each sound.

2 (🎧 3.24) **Listen and repeat the words. Is it a short vowel or a long vowel?**

A rhyme

3 (🎧 3.25) **Listen and say the rhyme. Copy the stress.**

I've got a hamster.
She's got a dog.
They've got a spider.
He's got a frog.
We've got a budgie.
You've got a cat.
Jack's got an elephant.
And Donna's got a rat.

A tongue twister

4 How fast can you say this?

Red lorry, yellow lorry. Red lorry, yellow lorry. Red lorry, yellow lorry.

Unit 4

/ɒ/ and /əʊ/

1 a (🎧 3.26) **Listen and repeat.**

> dog phone home comic song hockey
> mobile go don't got nose postman
> clock ocean box shop

b Put the words with the dog or the phone.

dog   *phone*

c (🎧 3.27) **Listen. If you hear 'a dog' word, say 'Woof, woof'.**

A rhyme

2 (🎧 3.28) **Listen and say the rhymes.**

Hickory, dickory dock
The mouse ran up the clock.
The clock struck one.
The mouse ran down.
Hickory, dickory dock.

A tongue twister

3 How fast can you say this?

A xylophone, a trombone, a saxophone, a mobile phone.

Unit 5

/ ʃ / and / s /

1 a 🎧 3.29 **Listen. Put the words with the shop or the cinema.**

> shop   cinema   shower   centre   office
> she   bus   brush   ocean   square   finish
> short   sofa   school   T-shirt   sport

shop

cinema

b 🎧 3.29 **Listen again and repeat.**

2 🎧 3.30 **Listen. If you hear the / ʃ / sound go up one step. When you reach the top, say 'Finish'.**

Start

A rhyme

3 🎧 3.31 **Listen and say the rhyme.**

I can see a shopping centre.
I can see a school.
Can you see a sports centre
And a swimming pool?

I can't see a station
And I can't see a shop.
But I can see a supermarket
Near the bus stop.

A tongue twister

4 How fast can you say this?

She sells sea shells on the sea shore.
The sea shells that she sells are sea shells, I'm sure.

Unit 6

Vowel sounds

1 a Which words have the same vowel sound? Match the words in A to the words in B.

A	B
1 blue	ears
2 mouth	bald
3 fat	tooth
4 short	hair
5 quite	brown
6 fair	red
7 beard	eyes
8 head	black

b 🎧 3.32 **Listen, check and repeat.**

Syllables

2 a How many syllables has each word got?

1 anything		7 clothes	
2 beautiful		8 jacket	
3 shoes		9 magazine	
4 trousers		10 eyes	
5 glasses		11 moustache	
6 usually		12 everyone	

1	2	3
shoes	jacket	anything

b 🎧 3.33 **Listen, check and repeat.**

A rhyme

3 🎧 3.34 **Listen and say the rhyme.**

Diddle diddle dumpling, my son John
Went to bed with his trousers on.
One sock off and one sock on.
Diddle diddle dumpling, my son John.

A tongue twister

4 How fast can you say this?

I scream. You scream. We all scream for ice cream.

Unit 1

1 How many of these are there in the picture?

- girls   - bags   - boys
- pens   - boxes   - pencils

2 What is on the teacher's desk?

3 a Find something in the picture beginning with these letters:

1 o   2 u   3 e   4 h   5 a

b How many things can you find beginning with these letters?

1 b   2 c   3 w   4 d

4 What letters of the alphabet can't you see on the poster?

5 What are the answers to the maths questions on the board?

Start

What is this continent?

What colours are in the UK flag?

What number is Toronto?

What number is the Sahara Desert?

What is this continent?

What colours are in the South African flag?

What is on the Argentinian flag?

What number is Cardiff?

What number is New York?

What number is Edinburgh?

Finish

What is on the Canadian flag?

What number is London?

What number is Hollywood?

Play the game

What number is the River Amazon?

What is this continent?

What is this continent?

What number is Tokyo?

What number is the Brazilian flag?

What is this continent?

What number is Sydney?

What number is Dublin?

What colours are in the Irish flag?

What is this continent?

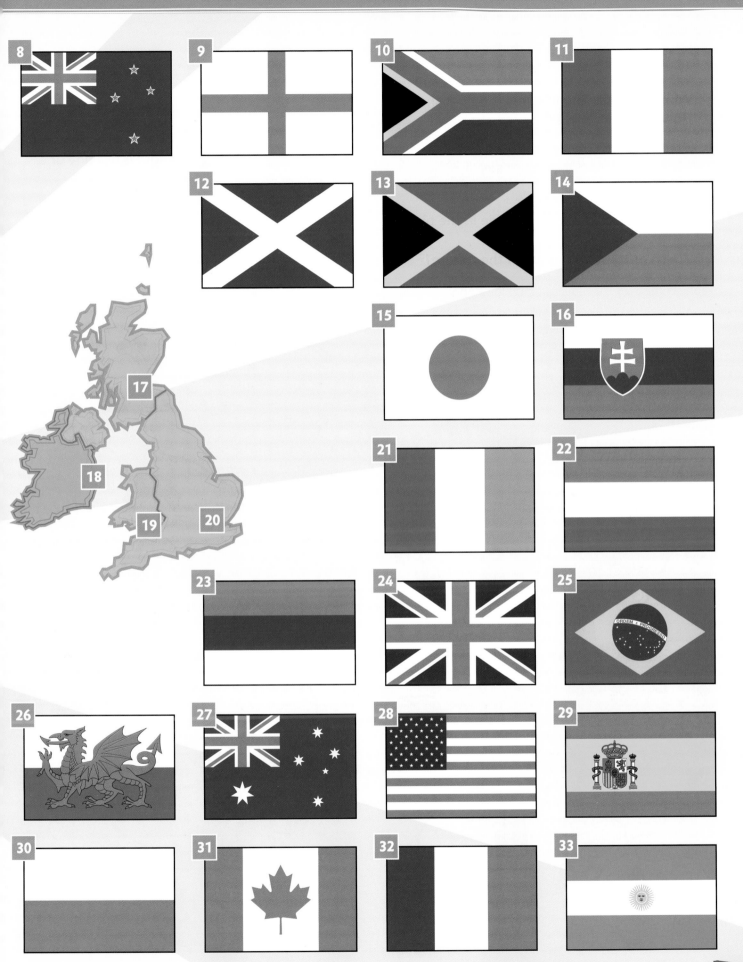

Unit 3

1 **Which of these animals are in the pet show? How many are there?**

a rat   a mouse   a hamster   a cat
a rabbit   a snake   a fish   a spider
a horse   a budgie   a dog   a frog

2 **What other animals can you see in the picture?**

3 **Which of these things are in the picture?**

a skateboard   a radio   a mobile phone
a remote-controlled car   a camera
MP3 player   a computer   a bike

4 **What colour are these:**

- the skateboard   - the car
- the horses   - the bike
- the fish   - the snake

5 **Who is wearing these things? Is it a boy or a girl?**

- a red cap
- a blue T-shirt
- a green T-shirt
- a yellow cap

Unit 4

1 a 🔊 3.35 Read and listen to the story. Find these things in the pictures.

Town Mouse   Country Mouse   a cow
a cart   a cat   a street   long grass

b Which mouse lives:

- on a farm?
- in a big house?

2 Put these things in the correct column.

a soft bed   wet grass   a cat   a noisy street
very big animals   dangerous   a dark bedroom
a clock   a hard bed   very quiet   lots of people

in the country   **in the town**

_____   _____

_____   _____

3 Are you a town mouse or a country mouse? What things do you like about your home?

Town Mouse and Country Mouse

One day Town Mouse visits his friend, Country Mouse. Country Mouse lives on a farm in the country.

'Hello, Town Mouse,' says Country Mouse. 'Come in.' He brings some food for his friend.

'Thank you,' says Town Mouse. He eats a bit of the food, but he doesn't like it. He doesn't eat food like this at home in the town.

Later Town Mouse goes to bed, but he doesn't go to sleep. The bed is hard and the bedroom is very dark and quiet.

In the morning Town Mouse and Country Mouse go for a walk. The grass is long and wet. Soon Town Mouse's legs and feet are wet.

'Do you like the country?' says Country Mouse.

'Well,' says Town Mouse 'I ….' Then suddenly, he sees a very big animal.

'Eek!' he shouts. Then he runs and hides in the long grass.

'What's that?' says Town Mouse.

'Oh, it's only a cow,' says Country Mouse, and he laughs.

But Town Mouse thinks: 'I don't like the country. I want to go back to the town.'

The next day the two mice see a cart on the road.

'Come on,' says Town Mouse. 'Let's go to my house in the town.' The two mice jump on the cart and travel to the town.

Town Mouse is very happy in the town, but Country Mouse doesn't like it. There are lots of people and carts in the streets. Town Mouse and Country Mouse go to a big house.

'This is my home,' says Town Mouse. 'Do you like it?'

'Well,' says Country Mouse. 'I …' Then suddenly, he hears a loud noise. BONG! BONG! BONG!

'Eek!' shouts Country Mouse. Then he runs and hides under a chair.

'What's that?' he says.

'Oh, it's only the clock,' says Town Mouse and he laughs.

Later Country Mouse goes to bed, but he doesn't go to sleep. The bed is very soft. The bedroom isn't very dark and the street is very noisy.

The next day they go for a walk, but they see a cat. The cat wants to eat the mice. Town Mouse and Country Mouse run back to the house.

'I don't like the town,' thinks Country Mouse. 'It's noisy and dangerous. I want to go home.'

Later he sees a cart from the farm. He jumps on the cart and says: 'Thank you, Town Mouse. Goodbye.'

Soon Country Mouse is in his little house on the farm again. 'I love my home,' he says.

Town Mouse sits in his big house in the town. 'I love my home,' he says.

Unit 5

1 a (🔊 3.36) **Read and listen to the story. Find these in the picture.**

> Finn Oonah Benan a cradle
> bread rolls stones the fire

b **Match the words to the people in the story.**

> bad good clever

2 Complete the sentences with the correct name.

1 _____ throws rocks at Benan.
2 _____ crosses the bridge to Ireland
3 _____ makes a cradle and gets into it.
4 _____ puts stones in the bread rolls.
5 _____ bites one of the stones.
6 _____ gives the baby a bread roll.
7 _____ runs back to Scotland.
8 _____ throws the rocks into the Atlantic Ocean.

3 Work in a group of three. Act the story.

Finn, The GIANT

Here's a story from long ago. Finn MacCool is a giant. He lives in Ireland. Finn is a good, strong giant. He lives with his wife, Oonah. Finn and his good, clever wife live on a hill near the sea.

On the other side of the sea is Scotland. A giant lives there, too. His name is Benan. He isn't a good giant. He's a big, bad giant. Finn doesn't like Benan. One day he throws some big rocks at Benan. Benan doesn't like Finn and he throws big rocks back. The rocks land in the sea between Ireland and Scotland.

Soon there are lots of rocks in the sea. The rocks make a bridge. Big, bad Benan starts to cross the bridge.

'Oh, no!' says Finn, and he runs home.

'What's wrong?' says Oonah when she sees her husband.

'Look,' he says. 'Here comes big, bad Benan! What can I do?'

'Quick,' says clever Oonah. 'Make a big baby's cradle.'

Finn collects some wood and makes a big cradle. 'Now get in the cradle and be quiet,' says Oonah. Then she collects some stones and makes some bread rolls. She puts stones into the rolls. But there is one roll with no stone in it.

Soon Benan arrives and he bangs on the door. 'Where's Finn?' he shouts.

'He isn't here,' says Oonah. 'There's only me and the baby at home.'

Benan looks at the cradle. 'That's a very big baby,' he says.

'Yes, just like his daddy,' says Oonah. 'Finn is a very big giant.'

'Oh,' says Benan. Then he sees the bread by the fire. 'Mmm. Those bread rolls smell very good,' he says. 'Can I have one?'

'Yes. Here you are,' says Oonah. She gives Benan a bread roll. There's a big stone in it.

'Thank you,' says Benan. He opens his big mouth and bites the bread roll. 'Ow!' he shouts. 'My teeth! This bread is very hard.'

'Oh,' says Oonah. 'Finn eats this bread every day. He likes it.' Then the baby starts to cry. 'Oh dear,' says Oonah. 'He's hungry. Here you are, baby. Here's a bread roll for you.'

'That baby's got very strong teeth,' says Benan. He doesn't know that there's no stone in the baby's bread roll. The baby eats the bread roll.

'Listen,' says Oonah. 'I think I can hear Finn outside now.'

'Oh, no,' thinks Benan. 'If this is Finn's baby, I don't want to meet Finn!' And he runs out of the house and back to the sea. As he crosses the bridge again, he picks up the big stones. He throws them far into the Atlantic Ocean. 'Finn can't follow me now,' he thinks.

But Finn doesn't want to follow Benan. He's happy in Ireland with his clever wife, Oonah.

Unit 6

1 a 🔊 3.37 **Read and listen to the story. Find these things in the picture.**

| the fox the crow the piece of cheese |

b Which animal:

- gets the cheese first?   - eats the cheese?

2 a Put the events in the correct order.

a The cheese falls.
b The fox says that the crow has got a beautiful voice.
c She flies up into a tree.
d The fox eats the piece of cheese.
e The crow picks up the piece of cheese.
f The crow opens her beak to sing.

b Why does the crow try to sing?

The Fox and the Crow

The fox is hungry. He's looking for food, but he can't find anything to eat. Then he sees something. It's a piece of cheese – nice, yellow cheese. The fox loves cheese.

He runs to get it, but then he sees a bird – a big black bird. It's a crow. The crow likes cheese, too. The big, black crow lands next to the cheese, picks it up in her beak and flies up into a tree.

The fox isn't happy. He's still hungry, but now he can't eat the piece of cheese. He can see it. It's in the crow's beak and the crow is sitting on a branch in the tree.

'I really want that piece of cheese,' thinks the fox. 'But how can I get it? I can't climb trees. And the crow can fly away.'

The fox is very clever and he has an idea. He walks to the tree and he looks up. The crow is sitting on a branch. She's holding the piece of cheese in her beak. She sees the fox, but she doesn't fly away. She knows that the fox can't get her. She's safe in the tree.

'Good morning, Mrs Crow,' says the fox and he smiles. 'How are you today?' The crow doesn't say anything. She can't speak because she's holding the piece of cheese in her beak.

'Isn't it a lovely day?' says the fox. 'The sun is shining. The birds are singing.'

The crow doesn't say anything.

'But you aren't singing,' says the fox. 'Why aren't you singing today, Mrs Crow? Everyone says that you've got a beautiful voice.'

Now everyone knows that the crow can't sing. She can only say 'Caw. Caw.' But the fox says: 'Please sing for me, Mrs Crow. I want to hear your beautiful voice.'

The crow wants to sing. She wants to have a beautiful voice.

'Please sing your beautiful song for me,' says the fox again.

The crow wants to sing. She opens her beak and says: 'Caw. Caw.'

But the fox isn't listening to her. When she opens her beak, the piece of cheese falls. It lands in front of the fox. He looks at the cheese. The crow looks at the cheese.

'Thank you,' says the fox. Then he picks up the piece of cheese – the nice, yellow cheese – and he eats it.

OXFORD
UNIVERSITY PRESS

Great Clarendon Street, Oxford, OX2 6DP, United Kingdom

Oxford University Press is a department of the University of Oxford.
It furthers the University's objective of excellence in research, scholarship,
and education by publishing worldwide. Oxford is a registered trade
mark of Oxford University Press in the UK and in certain other countries

© Oxford University Press 2013

The moral rights of the author have been asserted

First published in 2013

2022 2021 2020 2019

10 9 8 7

ISBN: 978 0 19 476455 1

Printed in China

This book is printed on paper from certified and well-managed sources

ACKNOWLEDGEMENTS

*The author and publisher are grateful to those who have given permission to adapt the
following copyright material:* p.85 adapted from *Classic Tales Beginner 2: The Town
Mouse and the Country Mouse,* retold by Sue Arengo © Oxford University Press
2008. p.86 adapted from *Classic Tales Beginner 2: Big Baby Finn,* retold by Sue
Arengo © Oxford University Press 2008.

*The author and publisher are very grateful to all the teachers who have offered their
comments and suggestions which have been invaluable in the development of Project
Fourth edition. We would particularly like to mention those who helped by writing
reports on Project:*

Slovenia: Jezerka Beškovnik, Katarina Grmek, Andreja Hazabent Habe, Jelena
Novak, Lidija Apat

Croatia: Lidija Branilović, Ivana Sauha, Ela Ivanić, Ana Pavić

Czech Republic: Jana Pecháčková, Petra Gušlová, Jana Ferancová, Šárka
Karpíšková, Marie Holečková

Slovakia: Mgr. Zuzana Laszlóová, Mgr. Bronislava Gulánová, Mgr. Peter Humay,
Ing. Zuzana Lennerová, Mgr. Katarina Tóth Mikócziová

Hungary: J. Tóth Judit, Csanády Szilvia, Papné Szalay Csilla, Bollog Melinda

Serbia: Sonja Preda Foljan, Ljiljana Ćuzović

*The author would like to thank all the people at, or engaged by, Oxford University Press,
who have contributed their knowledge, skills and ideas to producing this book.*

*The author would like to dedicate this book to his daughter, Mandy, and her three
children, Megan, Eloise and Dominic.*

Extra material (pp.82-83): Aradi László

The publisher would like to thank the following for permission to reproduce photographs:
Alamy Images pp15 (Skateboard/Markos Dolopikos), 15 (Manchester United
logo/Andrew Walters), 15 (Computer monitor/Alex Strokes), 24 (10 Downing
Street/Nathan King), 24 (221B Baker Street/Loop Images Ltd), 24 (Beatles
Abbey Road album cover/Pictorial Press), 24 (Penny Lane street sign/
Prisma Bildagentur AG), 36 (Students at lunch/MBI), 37 (Humpback whales/
Corey Ford), 37 (Duck/John McKenna), 37 (Bumblebee/David Cole), 37 (Tree
frog/H Lansdown), 37 (Brown bear/imagebroker), 48 (Netball match/Alan
Edwards), 48 (Boy takes part in the high jump/Sean Spencer), 60 (Modernistic
millennium clock in Royal Tunbridge Wells/Philip Bird), 60 (Shopping
arcade/Jon Arnold Images Ltd), 60 (Outdoor ice rink/Alex Segre), 63 (Digital
camera/Alamy Creativity), 72 (Portrait of boy/Corbis Flint), 72 (Portrait of boy/
dbimages); Bridgeman Art Library Ltd p73 (Sunday Afternoon on the Island
of La Grande Jatte, Seurat, Georges Pierre / The Art Institute of Chicago, IL,
USA); Corbis pp12 (Portrait of girl/Rob Lewine/Tetra Images), 18 (Smiling
woman outdoors/Mark Edward Atkinson/Tracey Lee/Blend Images), 18 (Teen
girl leaning against tree/Ron Nickel/Design Pics), 23 (Teen girl with mobile
phone/Auslöser), 23 (Boy using cell phone/Bruce Laurance/Blend Images),
25 (Meandering river/Adam Jones/Visual Unlimited), 35 (Student taking exam/
Ian Lishman/Juice Images), 35 (Chemistry class/Ian Lishman/Juice Images),
48 (Rugby match/Tim Clatyon/101010), 48 (Baseball game/Mark Goldman/
Icon SMI), 48 (Boy smiling/Kentaroo Tryman/Johner Images), 51 (Muddy bike/
Rolf Brenner), 60 (Girl with strawberries/Paul Barton), 63 (Male fishmonger/
Ocean), 72 (Fishing boats on beach/Jon Hicks), 72 (Teen girl/Nancy Ney),
72 (Singapore/Jon Hicks); Getty Images pp12 (Portrait of a country boy/Cultura/
Nick Daly), 12 (Smiling girl/KidStock), 14 (Girl with hands on hips/Andersen
Ross/Blend Images), 14 (Smiling boy/Rayes/Photodisc), 15 (Mountain bike/
Creative Crop), 16 (Portrait of girl and boy smiling/Rubberball), 17 (Portrait of
girl and boy smiling/Rubberball), 25 (Mianzimu Park/Feng Wei Photography),
25 (Ocean/Fred Froese), 25 (Europe map/Jon Schulte/Photographer's Choice),
36 (Teen girl portrait/Huntstock), 36 (Chinese boy/Stephen Marks), 36 (Young
boy smiling/Christine Schneider/Cultura), 36 (Girl smiling/Yellow Dog
Productions), 38 (Boy in classroom/Dominic DiSala), 38 (Smiling girl/Fabrice
LEROUGE), 48 (Ronnie O'Sullivan/Laurence Griffiths), 48 (Rory McIlroy/Sports
Illustrated), 48 (Smiling girl/Jessica Holden Photography), 60 (Young girl/
Tetra Images), 60 (Portrait of boy/Ana Lukascuk), 60 (Boy standing outdoors/
Camille Tokerud), 62 (Portrait of boy smiling/Purestock), 72 (Portrait of girl/
Soul/Lifesize), 72 (View from Fisherman's bastion/Romeo Reidl), 72 (Teen
boy/Granger Wootz), 72 (Abuja National Mosque/Irene Becker Photography);
iStockphoto pp (textured background/Hudiemm), 10 (notepad page/Brian
Adducci), 12 (identity documents/Edward Shaw), 13 (ad space/DNY59),
13 (maths/Vikram Raghuvanshi), 15 (footballs/Mark Murphy), 22 (torn paper/
Robyn Mackenzie), 24 (parcel/Kamo), 27 (scrapbooking/Natalia Bokach),
34 (blank cards/kyoshino), 35 (push pin/blackred), 35 (boy with molecules/
zorani), 36 (maths/Vikram Raghuvanshi), 36 (torn notepad page/hudiemm),
37 (jungle background/Alonzo Design), 39 (circuitboard/Steven Foley),
48 (sport background/Jamie Farrant), 49 (sheet music/Lisa Valder), 51 (sport
frame/woewchikyury), 55 (ad space/DNY59), 60 (bunting/PeskyMonkey),
61 (scroll/ajaykampani), 61 (linen canvas/Miroslav Boskov), 63 (map/pop_jop),
64 (notepad page/hudiemm), 72 (Earth/evirgen), 75 (magazine rack/Hande
Guleryuz Yuce); OUP pp12 (Boy smiling/Fuse), 15 (House/Paul Springett),
22 (Radio announcer/Corbis), 25 (Desert/Mark Phillips), 35 (football/
BananaStock), 36 (Children at school/Chris King), 37 (Elephants/Corbis/Digital
Stock), 72 (Blue Mosque/Photodisc), 75 (boys biking/Comstock), 82 (flags/
xiver), 83 (Argentina flag/ The Flag Institute) (Brazil, Czech Republic, Hungary,
Serbia Flags/ Whilhelmus Pictor) 82 (Slovakia, Spain Flags/ Vexillographer);
SuperStock p43 (Asian schoolgirls/Fancy).

Commissioned photography by: Gareth Boden pp4, 5, 7, 8, 12, 15, 16,
18 (grandparents, parents, uncle, Joe, Mel), 19, 22, 27, 28, 32, 35 (maths,
common room), 39, 41, 42, 43, 51, 56, 63, 64, 66, 70, 75.

Illustrations by: Piers Baker pp6 (ex.2), 18 (ex.4), 19, 41, 45, 52, 53 (ex.3b), 54, 56,
78 (ex.2), 79, 81; David Banks pp11 (ex.10), 14, 37 (ex.5), 53 (ex.5), 67, 69, 77,
78 (ex.3), 84; Moreno Chiacchiera/Beehive pp9 (ex.11), 15, 27, 51, 63, 71, 75,
85, 86, 87; Gary Davies p59; Paul Daviz front cover, Mickey Millie and Mut;
Fred van Deelen/The Organisation pp13 (ex.6), 25, 62, 82 (maps); James Hart/
Sylvie Poggio pp29, 33, 37 (ex.1&2), 49, 57, 65, 74, 76, 80; Chris Pavely pp6,
9 (ex.6), 10, 11 (ex.9), 16, 17, 18 (ex.1), 24 (Sherlock), 26, 28, 31 (ex.3b), 32, 34,
44, 50, 55, 61, 64, 70; Lisa Smith pp13 (ex.5), 40, 47.